*Ideas in the Drama*

# Ideas in the Drama

SELECTED PAPERS FROM THE ENGLISH INSTITUTE

EDITED WITH A FOREWORD BY JOHN GASSNER

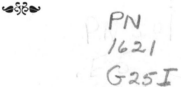

*Columbia University Press*

NEW YORK AND LONDON

FOR *Mark Van Doren*

# Foreword

A decade ago it would have required considerable temerity for scholars to consider the subject of "ideas" in literature, and to give serious consideration to the presence of ideas in the drama in recent years would have seemed downright quixotic—the last undisguised effort to do so in American scholarship appeared in 1946 when Eric Bentley published *The Playwright as Thinker*. That the English Institute should have devoted two conferences, in 1962 and 1963, to the subject may signify some relaxation of the reigning principle that the study of literature should be insulated against contamination by extraliterary and nonaesthetic considerations.

It is too soon to determine how far the restoration of a balance between aesthetic and nonaesthetic considerations will go. It is also too early to decide how rewarding the enterprise is going to prove. It is certain only that a reinstated interest in ideas would not bring scholarship back to the bad old habit of confusing intellectual intentions with artistic execution. Some questions that may be expediently slurred over will ultimately have to be answered—chiefly, what it is that constitutes an idea in a nonessayistic form of literature such as the drama and in what respects it is distinguishable from mere argument, demonstration, or propaganda. The fable, or *mythos,* as idea, characterization or orches-

tration of characters as idea, structure as idea, and texture, atmosphere, mood, and tonality as idea are aspects of the subject that
require substantial investigation and evaluation. Here and there
in the present work, beginning with Professor Arrowsmith's
stimulating paper, will be found investigations and evaluations
along these lines; neither exhaustive nor "final," they are partial
forays into an area of interest to which a large significance cannot
be denied without maiming criticism and scholarship. And our
subject, which cannot be compressed into a simple definition,
comes sufficiently into view; in our volume, drama of ideas, I
believe, manages to define itself gradually by example, qualifica-
tion, and extension.

The role of ideas as mere catalysts, in some instances, and as
elements in a complex chemical combination and transformation, in other instances, calls for discrimination and particulari-
zation. The writer who starts with a seemingly simple concept
is apt to end with a radically transformed one when a concept is
particularized and fleshed out. And if this is true of any sort of
creative endeavor, it is all the more likely to be the case in con-
sidering dramatic work, in which the author is not, as a rule,
speaking in his own voice but through his characters.

Plays, moreover, are affected by numerous factors that relate
the original text to the conditions of stage production. Alterations
made during the rehearsal and the tryout periods are normally
reflected in the final text that reaches the reader. Playwrights may
find the very meaning of their work altered quite against their
original, and perhaps better, judgment under the pressure of having to make a play viable on the stage for a particular audience, to

satisfy a particular stage director, or to suit the talent or disposition of an important performer. Even strong-minded playwrights have regularly succumbed to the conditions of "show business" and stage production, the dictation or persuasion of managers and directors, and the blandishments of star performers. A student of dramatic literature must indeed pick his way warily among ideas, even when these are professed and defined by the author himself. But not to venture among them at all is to overlook the nature of dramatic structure altogether, since a play is not a yarn but an action determined by theme. It is therefore with more confidence in the function of ideas in the drama than trepidation concerning their manifest dangers to crude playwrights and critics that I offer the papers selected for inclusion in this volume.

I must not close this foreword, however, without expressing considerable indebtedness to Professor Vivian Mercier of The City·College of New York. Professor Mercier directed the 1962 conference that contributed two important papers, his own essay and that of Professor William Arrowsmith of the University of Texas, to this collection. The conference on Ideas in the Drama over which I presided in 1963 was simply a continuation of the project provocatively started by Professor Mercier.

JOHN GASSNER

*Yale University*
*New Haven, Connecticut*
*March, 1964*

# Contents

*Ideas in the Drama*

# WILLIAM ARROWSMITH

◈

# A Greek Theater of Ideas

Several years ago I made a plea that scholars and critics should recover a feeling for what I called turbulence in Greek tragedy.[1] By turbulence I meant both "the actual disorder of experience as that experience gets into Greek drama" and "the impact of ideas under dramatic test." What I want to do here is to take up the turbulence of ideas, as I see those ideas expressed by Euripidean drama, with the purpose of showing that the Greeks possessed a theater which we should have no difficulty in recognizing as a genuine theater of ideas. By theater of ideas I do not mean, of course, a theater of intellectual *sententiae* or Shavian "talk" or even the theater of the sophist-poet; I mean a theater of dramatists whose medium of thought was the stage, who used the whole machinery of the theater as a way of *thinking*, critically and constructively, about their world.

In such a theater I assume that the emphasis will be upon ideas rather than character and that a thesis or problem will normally take precedence over development of character or heroism; that aesthetic or formal pleasure will be secondary to intellectual rigor and thought; and that the complexity of ideas presented may require severe formal dislocations or intricate blurrings of emotional modes and genres once kept artistically distinct. It is also likely that the moral texture of an action will be "difficult," and that

[1] See "The Criticism of Greek Tragedy," in *The Tulane Drama Review*, III, No. 3 (Spring, 1959), 31 ff.

moral satisfaction will not come easily or even at all; that
problems may be left unresolved; that is, that the effect of a play
may very well be discomfort or even pain, and that the purpose
of this discomfort will be to influence the social rather than the
individual behavior of the spectator. Beyond this, I would expect
such a theater to be commonly concerned with the diagnosis and
dramatization of cultural crisis, and hence that the universe in
which the dramatic action takes place would tend to be either
irrational or incomprehensible. All of these characteristics are, of
course, abstracted at random from the historical theater of ideas
from Hebbel to the present, but in their ensemble they serve to
give at least a general sense of the kind of theater of ideas I have
in mind.

That such a theater—so specifically modern and anti-traditional
a theater—existed among the Greeks is not, I believe, exactly an
article of faith among scholars and critics. To be sure, the Greek
theater, like any other great theater, made abundant use of ideas,
and the Athenians regarded the theater, not as entertainment, but
as the supreme instrument of cultural instruction, a democratic
*paideia* complete in itself. Aeschylus, for instance, uses ideas with
stunning boldness, showing in play after play how the great post-
Hesiodic world order could be compellingly and comprehensively
adapted to Athenian history and society; and his theater not only
provides a great, and new, theodicy, but dramatically creates the
evolving idea of Athens as the supreme achievement of the mind
of Zeus and the suffering of mankind. As for Sophocles, I am not
of those who believe that he, like Henry James, possessed a mind
so fine that no idea could violate it. In Oedipus, for instance, we
have Sophocles' image of heroic man, shorn of his old Aeschylean

confidence in himself and his world, and relentlessly pursuing the terrible new truth of his, and human, destiny. Oedipus looks into the abyss that yawns beneath him—the frightful knowledge of his nature which fifth-century man had learned from the war, the plague and the atrocities, the sophistic revolution, and the collapse of the old world-order—and dashes out his eyes at the unbrookable sight. Similarly in Sophocles' Ajax I think we are meant to see a somewhat earlier symbol of the old aristocratic ethos; caught in new and antiheroic circumstances which degrade him and make him ludicrous, Ajax consistently prefers suicide to a life of absurdity in an alien time.[2] But all this is merely to say that Sophocles, like Aeschylus, uses the perceptions of cultural crisis as framing dramatic ideas or symbolically, not that his theater is in any meaningful sense a theater of ideas. Clearly it is to Euripides —the innovator and experimentalist, the anti-traditional "immoralist" and "stage-sophist"—that we must look for any valid fifth-century theater of ideas.

That the second half of the fifth century B.C. was a period of immense cultural crisis and political convulsion is, fortunately for my purpose here, beyond any real doubt. The evidence itself needs only the barest rehearsal, but it should at least be *there,* the real though sketchy weather of my argument. Let me therefore brush it in.

There is, first of all, the breakdown of the old community, the overwhelming destruction of that mythical and coherent world-

---

[2] Compare Ajax' situation with Thucydides' statement in the Corcyraean excursus: "The ancient simplicity into which honor so largely entered was laughed down and disappeared."

order which Werner Jaeger has described so fully in *Paideia*.
Political convulsion—stasis and revolution—broke out everywhere.
If civil war was nothing new among the Greek city-states, civil
war on the fifth-century scale was absolutely unprecedented in its
savagery: city against city, man against man, father against son.
Under such conditions the whole kinship structure on which the
polis was theoretically and constitutionally founded was irre-
trievably weakened. In culture the sophistic revolution ushered in
something like a transvaluation of morals. In society there was
the rise of a new bourgeoisie provided with new sanctions and
new theories of human nature, as well as a politically conscious
proletariat. In the arts restless innovation was the rule, and
throughout the Hellenic world—in literature, thought, and politics—there took place a vast debate whose very terms vividly
report the schism in the culture, especially in the great argument
between *physis* (nature) and *nomos* (custom, tradition, and
law). Men begin to wonder now whether the laws of the state
and the state itself, once thought divinely established, are any
longer related to *physis* at large or to human *physis* in particular.
Thus the great experience of the late fifth century is what can be
called "the loss of innocence." Sophocles, Euripides, Aristophanes,
and Thucydides are all, each in his different way, haunted by the
disappearance of the old integrated culture and the heroic image
of man that had incarnated that culture. There is a new spirit of
divisiveness abroad in the Hellenic world; appearance and reality,
nature and tradition, move steadily apart under the destructive
pressure of war and its attendant miseries. Subjected to harsh
necessity, human nature now shows itself in a new nakedness, but

also in a startling new range of behavior, chaotic and uncontrollable.

How wrenching that convulsion was, how extreme and catastrophic, is told us by no less an authority than Thucydides himself:

So bloody was the march of the revolution [in Corcyra], and the impression which it made was the greater as it was one of the first to occur. Later on, one may say, the whole Hellenic world was convulsed. . . . The sufferings which revolution entailed upon the cities were many and terrible, such as have occurred and always will occur, as long as the nature of mankind remains the same; though in a severer or milder form, and varying in their symptoms, according to the variety of the particular cases. In peace and prosperity states and individuals have better sentiments, because they do not find themselves suddenly confronted with imperious necessities; but war takes away the easy supply of daily wants, and so proves a rough master that brings most men's characters to a level with their fortunes. Revolution thus ran its course from city to city, and the places which it arrived at last, from having heard what had been done before, carried to a still greater excess the refinement of their inventions, as manifested in the cunning of their enterprises and the atrocity of their reprisals. Words had to change their ordinary meaning and to take that which was now given them. Reckless audacity came to be considered the courage of a loyal ally; prudent hesitation, specious cowardice; moderation was held to be a cloak for unmanliness; ability to see all sides of a question inaptness to act on any. Frantic violence became the attribute of manliness; cautious plotting, a justifiable means of self-defence. The advocate of extreme measures was always trustworthy; his opponent a man to be suspected. . . . Even blood became a weaker tie than party, from the superior readiness of those united by the latter to dare everything without reserve; for such associations had not in view the blessings derivable from established institutions but were formed by ambition for their overthrow; and the confidence of their members in each other rested less on any religious sanction than upon complicity in crime. . . .

The cause of all these evils was the hunger for power arising from greed and ambition; and from these passions proceeded the violence of parties once engaged in contention. The leaders in the cities, each provided with the fairest professions, on the one side with the cry of political equality for the people, on the other of a moderate aristocracy, sought prizes for themselves in those public interests which they pretended to cherish, and, recoiling from no means in their struggles for ascendancy, engaged in the direct excesses; in their acts of vengeance they went to even greater lengths, not stopping at what justice or the good of the state demanded, but making the party caprice of the moment their only standard, and invoking with equal readiness the condemnation of an unjust verdict or the authority of the strong arm to glut the animosities of the hour. Thus religion was in honor with neither party, but the use of fair phrases to arrive at guilty ends was in high reputation. Meanwhile the moderate part of the citizenry perished between the two, either for not joining in the quarrel or because envy would not suffer them to escape.

Thus every form of evil took root in the Hellenic countries by reason of the troubles. The ancient simplicity into which honor so largely entered was laughed down and disappeared; and society became divided into camps in which no man trusted his fellow. To put an end to this, there was neither promise to be depended upon, nor oath that could command respect; but all parties dwelling rather in their calculation upon the hopelessness of a permanent state of affairs, were more intent upon self-defence than capable of confidence. In this contest the blunter wits were most successful. Apprehensive of their own deficiencies and of the cleverness of their antagonists, they feared to be worsted in debate and to be surprised by the combinations of their more versatile opponents, and so at once boldly had recourse to action; while their adversaries, arrogantly thinking that they should know in time, and that it was unnecessary to secure by action what policy afforded, often fell victims to their want of precaution.

Meanwhile Corcyra gave the first example of most of the crimes alluded to; of the reprisals exacted by the governed who had never experienced equitable treatment or indeed anything except outrage from their rulers—when their hour came; of the iniquitous resolves of those who desired to get rid of their accustomed poverty, and ardently coveted their neighbors' possessions; and lastly, of the savage and pitiless excesses into which men who had begun the struggle, not in a class but a party spirit, were hurried by their ungovernable passions. In the confusion into which life was now thrown in the cities, human nature, always rebelling against the law and now its master, gladly showed itself uncontrolled in passion, above respect for justice, and the enemy of all superiority; since revenge would not have been set above religion, and gain above justice, had it not been for the fatal power of envy. Indeed men too often take upon themselves in the prosecution of their revenge to set the example of doing away with those general laws to which all alike can look for salvation in their day of adversity, instead of allowing them to exist against the day of danger when their aid may be required.                (III, 82 ff. Trans. Crawley)

Every sentence of that account deserves to be read, slowly and meditatively, with due weight given to every phrase, every word, lest we underread, as we so often do with the classics, and translate the greatest cultural crisis of the Hellenic world into a parochial and ephemeral time of troubles. If Thucydides is to be trusted, the culture of his time had been shaken to the roots, and he feared for its survival.

How did this convulsion of a whole culture affect the idea of a theater as we find that idea expressed by Euripides?

The immediate, salient fact of Euripides' theater is the assumption of a universe devoid of rational order or of an order incomprehensible to men. And the influence of Aristotle is nowhere more obvious than in the fact that this aspect of Euripides' theater is the one least often recognized or acted upon by critics. Yet it is stated both explicitly and implicitly from play to play throughout Euripides' lifetime. "The care of god for us is a great thing," says the chorus of Hippolytus, "if a man believe it. . . . So I have a secret hope of someone, a god, who is wise and plans; / but my hopes grow dim when I see / the actions of men and their destinies. / For fortune always veers and the currents of life are shifting, / shifting, forever changing course." "O Zeus, what can I say?" cries Talthybius in *Hecuba.* "That you look on men and care? Or do we, holding that the gods exist, / deceive ourselves with unsubstantial dreams / and lies, while random careless chance and change / alone control the world?" Usually desperate, feeble, and skeptical in the first place, it is the fate of these hopes to be destroyed in action. In *Heracles* the fatal chaos of the moral universe is shown formally; a savage reversal which expresses the flaw in the moral universe splits the entire play into two contrasting actions connected only by sequence. Thus the *propter hoc* structure required by Aristotelian drama is in Euripides everywhere annulled by *created* disorder and formal violence. What we get is *dissonance, disparity, rift, peripeteia;* in Euripides a note of firm tonality is almost always the sign of traditional parody; of the false, the unreal, or lost innocence remembered in anguish. What this assumption of disorder means is: first, that form is not organic; second, that character is not destiny, or at best that only a part of it is; and third, that Aristotelian notions of responsibility, tragic flaw, and heroism are not pertinent.

The central dissonance assumes a variety of forms. But the commonest is a carefully construed clash between myth (or received reality) on the one hand, and fact (or experienced reality) on the other. Λόγῳ μέν . . . ἔργῳ δέ, as the Greeks put it, contrasting theory (*logos*) and fact (*ergon*), appearance (or pretence) and reality, legend and truth. In *Alcestis,* for instance, Euripides juxtaposes the traditional, magnanimous Admetus with the shabby egotist who results when a "heroic" character is translated into realistic fifth-century terms. By making Alcestis take Admetus at his own estimate, Euripides delays the impact of his central idea—the exposure of Admetus' *logos* by his *ergon*—until the appearance of Pheres, whose savage "realistic" denunciation of his son totally exposes the "heroic" Admetus. By a similar translation, Euripides' Odysseus becomes a demagogue of *realpolitik,* Agamemnon a pompous and ineffectual field marshal, and Jason a vulgar adventurer. It was, of course, this technique of realism, this systematic exposure and deflation of traditional heroism, which earned Euripides his reputation for debasing the dignity of the tragic stage. And in some sense the charge is irrefutable. Euripides' whole bent is clearly anti-traditional and realistic; his sense of rebelliousness is expressed beyond doubt by the consistency with which he rejects religious tradition, by his restless experiments with new forms and new music, and by his obvious and innocent delight in his own virtuosity—his superior psychology and his naturalistic stagecraft. With justifiable pride he might have seen himself as a dramatic pioneer, breaking new ground, and courageously refusing to write the higher parody of his predecessors which his world—and ours—have demanded of him. There must be, I imagine, very few theaters in the world where the man who writes of "people as they are" is automatically judged inferior to the man who writes of "people as they should be."

But it would be wrong to assume that realism was the whole story or that Euripides was drawn to realism because he knew it would offend the worthies of his day. For it was life, not Euripides, which had abandoned the traditional forms and the traditional heroism. What Euripides reported, with great clarity and honesty, was the widening gulf between reality and tradition; between the operative and the professed values of his culture; between fact and myth; between *nomos* and *physis;* between life and art. That gulf was the greatest and most evident reality of the last half of the fifth century, *the* dramatic subject par excellence, and it is my belief that the theater of Euripides, like Thucydides' history, is a radical and revolutionary attempt to record, analyze and assess that reality in relation to the new view of human nature which crisis revealed. To both Thucydides and Euripides, the crisis in culture meant that the old world order with its sense of a great humanity and its assumption of an integrated human soul was irrecoverably gone. The true dimensions of the human psyche, newly exposed in the chaos of culture, forbade any return to the old innocence or heroism. Any theater founded on the old psyche or the old idea of fate was to that extent a lie. The task imposed upon the new theater was not merely that of being truthful, of reporting the true dimensions and causes of the crisis, but of coping imaginatively and intellectually with a change in man's very condition.

It is for this reason that Euripides' theater almost always begins with a severe critique of tradition, which necessarily means a critique of his predecessors. Such programmatic criticism is what we expect from any new theater, and in the case of Greek theater, where the dramatist is official *didaskalos,* charged with the *paideia* of his people, it was especially appropriate. Aeschylus and Sophocles were not merely great theatrical predecessors; they were the moral tutors of Athens and their versions of the myths embodied, as nothing else did, the values of tradition and the old *paideia.* Given such authority and power, polemic and criticism were only to be expected, the only possible response; indeed, were it not for the fact that Euripides' criticism has generally been construed as cultural *lèse-majesté,* the point would hardly be worth making. When Shakespeare or Ibsen or Shaw or Brecht criticizes the theater of his immediate predecessors, we applaud; this is what we expect, the aggressive courage a new theater requires. When Euripides does it, it becomes somehow sacrilege, a crime against the classics. We respond, if at all, with outraged traditionalism, automatically invoking that double standard which we seem to reserve for the classics, that apparent homage which turns out to be nothing but respect for our own prejudices.

In Euripides' case, the prejudice is usually justified by the argument that Euripides' criticism of his predecessors is destructive and negative; that his attack on the old order is finally nothing but the niggling rage for exposure, devoid of constructive order. If this argument were sound, it would be impressive; but it is not enough to offer on Euripides' behalf the reply which Morris Cohen is said to have made to a student who accused him of destroying his religious beliefs: "Young man, it is recorded of Heracles that he was required only to *clean* the Augean stables." Not, that is, if we are serious in maintaining that Euripides was a great dramatist. Negative criticism of dead tradition and inert values is often of positive therapeutic effect, but no really great dramatist, it seems to me, can escape the responsibility for imaginative order. Actually the charge that Euripides is negative is based upon misreading of the plays. For one thing Euripides did not always expose myth and tradition; this is his bias, to be sure, but there are exceptions in which the received myth and its values are used to criticize contemporary reality and public policy. The obvious example is the *Trojan Women*. A more revealing instance is the *Iphigenia in Tauris,* in which the cult of Artemis of Brauron is reestablished by Athena at the close of the play in order to lay bare the immense human "blood sacrifice" of the Peloponnesian War.

The point here, I believe, is both important and neglected. Let me try to restate it. Euripides' favorite technique for demonstrating the new dissonance in Athenian culture, the disparity between putative values and real values, is simply realism of the pattern λόγῳ μέν . . . ἔργῳ δέ. But it is balanced at times by the converse technique—allowing the myth to criticize the everyday reality—ἔργῳ μέν . . . λόγῳ δέ. And these exceptions are important, since they show us that Euripides' realism is not a matter of simple anti-traditionalism, but consistent dramatic technique. What is basic is the mutual criticism, the mutual exposure that occurs when the incongruities of a given culture— its actual behavior and its myth—are juxtaposed in their fullness. That this is everywhere the purpose of Euripidean drama is clear in the very complaints critics bring against the plays: their tendency to fall into inconsistent or opposed parts (*Heracles, Andromache*); their apparent multidimensionality (*Alcestis, Heracles*), the frequency of the *deus ex machina.* This last device is commonly explained by a hostile criticism as Euripides' penchant for archaism and aetiology, or as his way of salvaging botched plays. Actually it is *always* functional, a part of the very pattern of juxtaposed incongruities which I have been describing. Thus the appearance of any god in a Euripidean play is invariably the sign of *logos* making its epiphany, counterpointing *ergon*.

Most Euripidean gods appear only in order to incriminate themselves (or a fellow god), though some—like Athena in the *Iphigenia in Tauris*—criticize the action and the reality which the action mirrors. But it is a variable, not a fixed, pattern, whose purpose is the critical counterpointing of the elements which Euripides saw everywhere sharply and significantly opposed in his own culture: myth confronted by behavior, tradition exposed by, or exposing, reality; custom and law in conflict with nature. What chiefly interested him was less the indictment of tradition, though that was clearly essential, than the *confrontation,* the *dramatic juxtaposition,* of the split in his culture. This was his basic theatrical perception, *his* reality, a perception which makes him utterly different from Aeschylus and Sophocles, just as it completely alters the nature of his theater.

Is that theater merely analytical then, a dramatic description of a divided culture? I think not. Consider this statement: "As our knowledge becomes increasingly divorced from real life, our culture no longer contains ourselves (or only contains an insignificant part of ourselves) and forms a social context in which we are not 'integrated.' The problem thus becomes that of again reconciling our culture with our life, by making our culture a living culture once more. . . ." That happens to be Ionesco on Artaud, but it could just as well be Euripides' description of the nature and purpose of his own theater. The reconciliation of life and culture is, of course, more than any theater, let alone a single dramatist, can accomplish; and it is perhaps enough that the art of a divided culture should be diagnostic, should describe the new situation in its complexity. Only by so doing can it redefine man's altered fate. It is my own conviction that Euripidean theater is critical and diagnostic, and that, beyond this, it accepts the old artistic burden of constructive order, does not restrict itself to analysis alone. But what concerns me at the moment is the way in which his basic theatrical perceptions altered his theater.

First and most significant after the destruction of *propter hoc* structure is the disappearance of the hero. With the sole exception of *Heracles*—Euripides' one attempt to define a new heroism— there is no play which is dominated by the single hero, as is Sophocles' *Oedipus* or *Ajax*.

Corresponding to the disappearance of the hero is Euripides' "fragmentation" of the major characters. What we get is typically an agon or contest divided between two paired characters (some- times there are three): Admetus and Alcestis; Jason and Medea; Hippolytus and Phaedra; Andromache and Hermione; Pentheus and Dionysus, etc. In such a theater, the Aristotelian search for a tragic hero is, of course, meaningless. But the significance of the fragmentation is not easy to assess; it is not enough to say merely that Euripides was temperamentally drawn to such conflict be- cause they afforded him opportunities for psychological analysis. What is striking about the consistently paired antagonists one finds in Euripides is, I think, their obsessional nature. They function like obsessional fragments of a whole human soul: Hippolytus as chastity, Phaedra as sexuality. The wholeness of the old hero is now represented divisively, diffused over several characters; the paired antagonists of the Euripidean stage thus represent both the warring modes of a divided culture and the new incompleteness of the human psyche. Alternatively, as in the *Bacchae,* they embody the principles of conflicting ideas: Pentheus as *nomos,* Dionysus as *physis.*

This fragmentation is also the sign of a new psychological interest. That the convulsion of the late fifth century had revealed new dimensions in the human psyche is sharply expressed by Thucydides, and just as sharply by Euripides. Indeed, Euripides' interest in abnormality and mental derangement is so marked that critics have usually seen it as the very motive of his drama. This, I think, is a mistake. The interest in psychology is strong, but it is always secondary; the real interest lies in the analysis of culture and the relationship between culture and the individual. If I am correct in assuming that Euripides' crucial dramatic device is the juxtaposition and contrast of *logos* and *ergon,* then it follows that the characters of his plays must bear the burden of the cultural disparity involved. I mean: if a myth is bodily transplanted from its native culture to a different one, then the characters of the myth must bear the burden of the transplantation, and that burden is psychological strain. Consider, for example, Euripides' Orestes, a man who murders his mother in an Argos where civil justice already exists; or the heroic Jason translated into the context of a fifth-century Corinth; or an Odysseus or Hermione or Electra cut off from the culture in which their actions were once meaningful or moral, and set in an alien time which *immoralizes* or *distorts* them. The very strain that Euripides succeeds in imposing upon his characters is the mark of their modernity, their involvement in a culture under similar strain. And it is the previously unsuspected range of the human psyche, the discovery of its powers, its vulnerability to circumstance, its incompleteness, and its violence, that interest Euripides, not the psychological process itself. The soliloquy in which Medea meditates the murder of her children is much admired; but

Euripides' dramatic interest is in the collapse or derangement of culture—the gap between *eros* and *sophia*—that makes the murder both possible and necessary.

Side by side with cultural strain is the striking loneliness of the Euripidean theater. Loneliness is, of course, a feature of traditional tragedy, but the difference between Euripides and his predecessors in this respect is marked. In Aeschylus the loneliness of human fate is effectively annulled by the reconciliation which closes trilogies and creates a new community in which god and man become joint partners in civilization. In Sophocles the sense of loneliness is extremely strong, but it is always the distinguishing mark of the hero, the sign of the fate which makes him an outcast, exiled from the world to the world's advantage and his own anguish. But in Euripides loneliness is the common fate. Insofar as the characters are fragmented and obsessional, their loneliness is required. The one thing they normally cannot do is communicate, and typically, even such communications as occur (for instance, Heracles' moving reunion with his children) are liable to almost certain destruction by the malevolence of fate. Again and again Euripides gives us those exquisite, painterly groupings which stress the impassable gulf which separates the old from the young, man from god, woman from man, and even hero from hero. The climax of the *Heracles* comes when Heracles, touched by Theseus' *philia,* makes his great decision to live; but the understanding is then immediately and deliberately clouded as Theseus fails to understand the enormous range of his friend's new heroism. The touch is typically and revealingly Euripidean. The gulf seems to close only to widen out again.

From the point of view of traditional tragedy nothing is more strikingly novel than the Euripidean fusion and contrast of comic and tragic effects. Thus at any point in a tragedy the comic, or more accurately, the pathetic or ludicrous, can erupt with poignant effect, intensifying the tragic or toughening it with parody. Nor is this a device restricted to Euripides' so-called "romantic" plays or his tragicomedies; it occurs even in the most powerful and serious tragedies. Tiresias and Cadmus in the *Bacchae,* for instance, are seen simultaneously as tragic and comic, that is, directly pathetic and incongruous: two old mummers of ecstasy; they try to dance for Dionysus as the god requires, but their bodies, like their minds, are incapable of expressing devotion except as a ludicrous mimicry. Aegeus, in *Medea,* has puzzled traditional interpretation from Aristotle on, precisely because he is Euripides' pathetic and ironic embodiment of Athens—that Athens which the chorus hails later as the place

> where Cypris sailed,
> and mild sweet breezes breathed along her path,
> and on her hair were flung the sweet-smelling garlands
> of flowers of roses by the Lovers, the companions
> of Wisdom, her escort, the helpers of men
> in every kind of *arete.*

The irony is not, of course, the cutting irony of exposure, but the gentler irony that comes when *logos* and *ergon* of things not too far apart are juxtaposed: we feel it as a light dissonance. Which is merely another way of saying that the new element of the comic in Euripidean tragedy is just one more instance of the dramatist's insistence upon preserving the multiplicity of possible realities in the texture of his action. In the traditional drama, such dissonance is rightly avoided as an offence against seriousness and tragic dignity; Euripides significantly sees both tragedy and comedy as equally valid, equally necessary. A drama of truth will contrive to contain them both; the complex truth requires it.

It is for this same reason that Euripides accentuates what might be called the multiple moral dimension of his characters. Every one of them is in some sense an exhibit of the sophistic perception that human character is altered by suffering or exemption from suffering; that every human disposition contains the possibilities of the species for good or evil. Aristotle objects, for instance, that Euripides' Iphigenia changes character without explanation. And so, in fact, she does, and so does Alcmene in *Heraclidae*. They change in this way because their function is not that of rounded characters or "heroes" but specifications of the shaping ideas of the play. Besides, if Heraclitus was right, and character is destiny, then the complex or even contradictory destiny which Euripidean drama assumes and describes must mean complex and contradictory characters. But the one kind of character which Euripides' theater cannot afford is that spendid integrated self-knowledge represented by the "old fantastical Duke of dark corners" in *Measure for Measure;* Euripides' theater is all Angelos, Lucios, and Claudios—average, maimed, irresolute, incomplete human nature. The case of Heracles himself, the most integrated hero Euripides ever created, is darkened by Euripides' insistence that we observe, without passing judgment, that even the culture-hero has murder in his heart. This fact does not, of course, compose a tragic flaw, but rather what Nietzsche called "the indispensable dark spring" of action. Moral judgment is, as Euripides tried to show, no less precarious and difficult than the comprehensive description of reality. How could it be otherwise?

This does not mean that Euripides avoids judgment or that his plays are attempts to put the problematic in the place of dramatic resolution. It means merely that his theater everywhere insists upon scrupulous and detailed recreation of the complexity of reality and the difficulty of moral judgment. The truth is concealed, but not impenetrably concealed. There can be little doubt, for instance, that Euripides meant his *Medea* to end in a way which must have shocked his contemporaries and which still shocks today. His purpose was, of course, not merely to shock, but to force the audience to the recognition that Medea, mortally hurt in her *eros,* her defining and enabling human passion, must act as she does, and that her action has behind it, like the sun, the power of sacred *physis.* There is no more savage moral oxymoron in Greek drama. But if Euripides here speaks up for *physis* against a corrupt *nomos,* he is capable elsewhere of defending *nomos* and insisting that those who prostrate themselves before *physis,* like the Old Nurse in Hippolytus, are the enemies of humanity. Necessity requires submission, but any necessity that requires a man to sacrifice the morality that makes him human, must be resisted to the end, even if it cost him—as it will—his life. Better death than the mutilation of his specifically human skill, that *sophia* which in Euripides is mankind's claim to be superior to the gods and necessity. Only man in this theater makes morality; it is this conviction, the bedrock classical conviction, that provides the one unmistakable and fixed reference-point in Euripides' dramatic world. Above that point all truths are purposely played off against one another in endless and detailed exactness of observation.

Within this new context of changed reality, Euripides' whole theater of ideas is set.

Several examples.

The *Iphigenia in Tauris* is a play commonly classified as romantic or escapist melodrama, and seems at first, or even second, sight extremely remote from the theater of ideas. Aristotle, for instance, particularly admired its elegant finish and its tightness of structure—especially its famous recognition scene—and he talks about it with the enthusiasm a nineteenth-century critic might have shown for a good "well-made" play. Smooth, urbane, and exciting, the play appears to be pure entertainment, lively and sophisticated but without a thought in its head. Clearly not tragic, its plot is as improbable as it is skillful; situation clearly counts for a great deal, characterization for very little. None of the leading characters, for instance, is given more than deft, generalizing traits, and the very slightness of the characterization draws attention to the virtuosity of the plot and the remarkable facility of execution.

But the romantic atmosphere is by no means absolute; again and again Euripides intrudes into this artificial world the jarring dissonance of a harsh contemporary reality. Quite deliberately, and with odd effect, he evokes and remembers the real war: the vision of the dead and the doomed; the illusion of ambition and the deceptive hope of empire; the exile's yearning for home; the bitter image of a Hellas at peace, remembered with longing from the impossible distance of the present. *Logos* set against *ergon;* form in partial conflict with subject; romantic myth undercut by, and therefore intensifying in turn, the actual world, as though the story of Cinderella were suddenly revealed as set on the outskirts of Auschwitz. If this play is melodrama, it is melodrama subtly but sensibly tilted toward the experience of national tragedy and exploiting that experience symbolically.

Symbolically how? It is perhaps easy for moderns to misunderstand or overread. But I wonder what Athenian, even the most insensitive, could have failed to grasp or respond to the image which this play sets before him, especially in the light of that experience of war which the play so powerfully exploits. *A sister dedicates her brother to death by the sword.* It seems perhaps melodramatic to moderns but, unless I am badly mistaken, that symbolism is directly addressed to the experience—and the conscience—of a people who, for nearly twenty years, had suffered all the horrors of fratricidal war. The symbolism is available and familiar, and it culminates naturally in the great recognition scene, when Iphigenia, on the point of butchering her brother Orestes, suddenly discovers his true identity. For this scene the whole play was built, and its quite remarkable power is ultimately based, I think, upon the explosive liberation of love which reunites a family or a people grown hostile, estranged, and unfamiliar. Behind the recognition of brother and sister in the play lies a people's recognition, a recognition of *kind*. For Argos, read Hellas; for the history of the house of Atreus, the history of Hellas. What is war but blood sacrifice? Why, the play asks, should Greeks kill Greeks? And to give his argument further point, Euripides introduces Athena to establish in Attica the cult of the civilized Artemis who will put an end to human sacrifice and, by implication, the needless butchery which is war. The symbolism is, of course, the more effective for being unobtrusive, but once felt, it drastically alters the experience of the play. What seems at first romantic escape becomes confrontation and recognition, a true tragicomedy in which the tragic shapes the comic or romantic and the romantic gives poignancy to the tragic. In short, the kind of play we might have expected from the dramatist of the *Alcestis* and the humanist of the *Trojan Women*. Admittedly a fresh political interpretation of its major symbolism does not transform the *Iphigenia in Tauris* into a true drama of ideas; but the existence of a deeply serious and critical intent in a play universally regarded as Euripides' most frivolous "entertainment," is indicative of the dramatist's bent in the "darker" plays.

In the *Orestes,* for instance. Here, if anywhere in Euripides' work, the contrast between *logos* and *ergon* is structural and crucial. The play falls abruptly into two distinct parts. *Ergon* is represented by the body of the play proper, a freely invented account of the events which followed Orestes' matricide; *logos,* by the concluding epiphany of Apollo, an archaizing *deus ex machina,* in which the god foretells the known mythical futures of the characters. These two parts are enjambed with jarring dissonance, since the characters as developed in the play and their mythical futures as announced by Apollo are incompatible. Through this device the play becomes problematic: the spectator is literally compelled, it seems, to choose between his own experience of the play and Apollo's closing words, between *ergon* and *logos,* behavior and myth. Moreover, the choice is a hard one;

for, if the experience of the play proper is of almost unbearable bitterness and pessimism, Apollo's arrangements are foolish and traditional to the point of unacceptability. In short, impasse, or so at first sight it might seem. But here, as so often in Euripides, a crux or problem or impasse is the dramatist's way of *confronting* his audience with the necessity of choosing between apparently antithetical realities or positions (Hippolytus or Phaedra? Pentheus or Dionysus? *Physis* or *nomos*? Cold expedience or passionate *eros*? Barbarian or Greek? Victim or oppressor? *Logos* or *ergon*?).[3] Almost without exception, these seemingly necessary choices are finally illusory alternatives, the dramatist's device for stimulating his audience and forcing it on to the critical perception which underlies and comprehends the alternatives, unifying them in a single, complex, synthetic judgment—the judgment which holds each play together and for which the plays were written in the first place. That Euripides' critics have so seldom managed to arrive at this final judgment would seem to indicate that his theatrical strategies were ineffective; on the other hand, Euripides' critics have usually assumed that his consistency of technique necessarily meant a consistent failure to write correct traditional tragedy in the (imagined) manner of Sophocles.

Certainly the impasse between *logos* and *ergon* in the *Orestes* is apparent only. What resolves it is a common purpose in both

[3] A dramatic adaptation, I believe, of Protagoras' *antilogoi* (the rhetorical technique of first attacking and then defending a thesis, or of antithetical theses). Thucydides' method of contrasting set speeches (the Mytilenean debate, for instance) is an historian's adaptation of the *antilogoi* and a way of indicating, between the lines, by what is omitted and shared by both speakers, the crucial spoken and unspoken assumptions of politics and ethics. So too in the case of Euripides.

parts—an ascending curve of exposure, first of the "heroic"
Orestes who killed his mother and tried to kill Helen, and then
of the traditionally "wise" Apollo who drove Orestes to matricide.
The exposures are, in fact, mutual and cumulative, compelling us
to see that if Orestes, by any human standard of morality, is mad,
Apollo is utterly insane (for madness or incompetence in a god,
and a god of radiant reason at that, is a fortiori more dangerous
than in a mortal). *Logos* and *ergon,* apparently contradictory, are
in fact complementary: depraved and immoral human action in
the play proper is mirrored and sanctioned by the callous folly
of heaven and the brutality of the myth; Orestes and Apollo
mutually create, mutually deserve, each other: murderers both.
Man and god project each other; myth influences behavior, and
behavior in turn shapes the myth in a vicious circle of moral
deterioration. If from this perspective we ask why Euripides
freely invents the story of Orestes instead of recreating the traditional matricide, the answer is immediately clear: because he
wants to demonstrate through the abortive attempt to kill Helen
—a crime in which Apollo significantly plays no part—that
Orestes is a murderer born, a man who kills not from necessity
but in *freedom,* out of his sickness and hatred. Having demonstrated this, Euripides can proceed to the complementary exposure
of Apollo, a god made in the image of Orestes.

Produced just half a century after Aeschylus' *Oresteia,* Euripides' *Orestes* is not only an indictment of the Aeschylean myth,
its values and its hero, but a savage critique of Hellenic society in
the last decade of the fifth century. If the impasse between *logos*
and *ergon* is, as I claim, resolved by a continuous mutual exposure, the purpose of that exposure is a complex and profoundly

bitter cultural statement. Euripides seems to be saying something like this: A society whose sacred legend is embodied in a god like Apollo and a man like Orestes runs the risk that its citizens may emulate the myth, revive it, in their own political behavior. That is, Athens and Greek society generally are in danger of realizing their own myths, of at last reconciling *logos* and *ergon*, myth and conduct, in a new synthesis of murderous brutality and insanity—the worst myth fused now with the worst behavior. In earlier plays Euripides critically contrasted myth and behavior with the aim of letting the better expose the worse; here, in the bitterest play of all, he shows how bad behavior and bad myth interact for the defeat of culture and communal life.

That this bleak conclusion is the purpose of the play is supported by the systematic desolation which Euripides visits upon every aspect of moral and political behavior. Thus there is not a character in the play who is not defined either by inhuman devotion to sound principle, by patient treachery, or by nightmare loyalty of complicity or stupidity. Every moral word is consistently inverted or emptied of its meaning, as the action proceeds from madness to "honorable" murder on a wave of sickening heroic rhetoric. As for justice, if Orestes creates none, he gets none either; for human justice here is merely power politics or mob passion, and Apollo rules in heaven. Between health and sickness, heroism and depravity, morality and immorality, every distinction is removed. Politics is either brutal power or demagoguery; the only honorable motives are self-interest and revenge. In short, the world of the *Orestes* is indistinguishable from the culture in convulsion described by Thucydides; point for point, Euripides and Thucydides confirm each other. And, presumptuous or not, I am tempted to see in this frightening play Euripides' apocalyptic vision of the final destruction of Athens and Hellas, or of that Hellas to which a civilized mind could still give its full commitment. In the house of Atreus we have the house of Hellas: the great old aristocratic house, cursed by a long history of fratricidal blood and war, brought down in ruin by its degenerate heirs.

Finally, consider the *Medea*. Traditionally classified as psychological tragedy, it is better interpreted as a genuine drama of ideas. Superficially it is a critique of relations between men and women, Greeks and barbarians, and of an *ethos* of hard, prudential self-interest as against passionate love. At a profounder level it is a comprehensive critique of the quality and state of contemporary culture. Like the *Bacchae,* Euripides' other great critique of culture, the *Medea* is based upon a central key term, *sophia*. Inadequately translated "wisdom," *sophia* is an extremely complex term, including Jason's cool self-interest, the magical and erotic skills of the sorceress Medea, and that ideal Athenian fusion of moral and artistic skills which, fostered by *eros,* creates the distinctive *arete* of the civilized polis. This third sense of *sophia*—nearly synonymous with "civilization" and specifically including the compassion[4] for the suppliant and the oppressed for which Athens was famous and which Aegeus significantly shows to Medea—is the standard by which the actions of Jason and Medea are to be judged. Thus the vivid harmony of *eros* and

[4] Cf. Euripides' *Electra*, 294–96, where Orestes says: "Compassion is found in men who are *sophoi,* never in brutal and ignorant men. And to have a truly compassionate mind is not without disadvantage to the *sophoi*."

*sophia* which Athens represents is precisely what Jason and Medea are not. Jason's calculating, practical *sophia* is, lacking *eros,* selfish and destructive; Medea's consuming *eros* and psychological *sophia* (an emotional cunning which makes her a supreme artist of revenge) is, without compassion, maimed and destructive. They are both destroyers, destroyers of themselves, of others, of *sophia,* and the polis.[5] And it is this *destructiveness* above all else which Euripides wants his audience to observe: the spirit of brutal self-interest and passionate revenge which threatens both life and culture, and which is purposely set in sharp contrast to life-enhancing Athens where the arts flourish, where *eros* collaborates with *sophia,* and where creative *physis* is gentled by just *nomoi.* Behind Jason and Medea we are clearly meant to see that spreading spirit of expedience and revenge which, unchecked by culture or religion, finally brought about the Peloponnesian War and its attendant atrocities. For it cannot be mere coincidence that a play like this was performed in the first year of the war.

What of Medea herself? Upon our understanding of her depends the final interpretation of the play. Thus those who find in Medea a barbarian woman whose lack of self-control, hunger for revenge, and male courage set her in firm contrast to the Corinthian women of the chorus, with their Greek praise of *sophrosunē* and their fear of excess, usually see the play as a psychological tragedy of revenge. Against this interpretation there

[5] Just as Medea and Jason between them destroy Creon and his daughter Glauke, so Medea, once she is domiciled in Athens, will attempt to murder Theseus, the son whom Aegeus so passionately desires—a fact which Athenians could be expected to know and hold against Medea, especially in view of Aegeus' generosity to her. Wherever Medea goes, the polis, as represented by the ruling family, is threatened.

are decisive arguments. For one thing, Euripides takes pains to show that Medea is not at all pure barbarian femininity, but rather a barbarian woman who has been partially and imperfectly Hellenized. Thus Medea's first appearance is an intentionally striking one, dominated by her attempt to pass for Greek, to say the right thing; she talks, in fact, the stock language of Greek women, *hēsuchia* and *sophrosunē*. Now this may be a pose, but it may just as well be genuine cultural imitation, the sort of thing a barbarian woman in Corinth might be expected to do. But the point is important for, if I am right, this play records the loss of the civilized skills through the conflict of passion; and for this reason Euripides first shows us his Medea making use of those civilized virtues which, in the throes of passion, she promptly loses, reverting to barbarism. Euripides' point is not that Medea *qua* barbarian is different in nature from Greek women, but that her inhibitions are weaker and her passions correspondingly nearer the surface. Thus she can very quickly be reduced to her essential *physis,* and it is this nakedness of *physis,* shorn of all cultural overlay, that Euripides wants displayed. Unimpeded *eros* (or unimpeded hatred) can be shown in Medea with a concentration and naturalness impossible in a Greek woman, not because Greek women were less passionate, but because their culture required them to repress their passions. If culture is truly effective, the control of passion eventually becomes true self-mastery (*sophrosunē*); where culture is less effective or out of joint (as in the Corinth of this play), *physis* is checked only by fear, and reveals itself in resentment of the punishing authorities and ready sympathy with those who rebel against them. Hence the profound resentment which the chorus in this play feels against male domination. This—and not mere theatrical convention or necessity—is why Medea can so easily convince the chorus to become her accomplices in her "crusade" against Jason and male society. Their control over their passions, while greater than Medea's perhaps, is still inadequate and precarious (as their bitter resentment of men makes clear); and Medea's revenge arouses their fullest sympathy, just as war evokes the barbarian in an imperfectly civilized man. And this is Euripides' point, that "one touch of nature" makes kin of Hellene and barbarian. In Medea's barbarism we have a concentrated image of human *physis* and a symbol of the terrible closeness of all human nature to barbarism. In her inadequate *sophrosunē* and her imperfect *sophia* is represented the norm of Hellenic, and most human, society. Thus when Jason cries out, "No Greek woman would have dared this crime," we are meant, not to agree, but to wonder and doubt, and finally to disbelieve him.

The validity of that doubt and disbelief is immediately confirmed by the appearance of the golden chariot of the Sun in which Medea makes her escape to Athens. In this chariot Euripides does two related things: he first restates, vividly and unmistakably, the triumph of Medea over Jason, and secondly he provides the whole action with a symbolic and cosmological framework which forces the private *agon* of Jason and Medea to assume a larger public significance. And by showing Medea, murderess and infanticide, as rescued by the Sun himself—traditionally regarded as the epitome of purity, the unstained god who will not look upon pollution—he drives home his meaning with the shock of near sacrilege. As for the chariot of the Sun, it is the visible cosmic force which blazes through Medea's motives and which her whole *pathos* expresses: the blinding force of life itself, stripped of any mediating morality or humanizing screen; naked, unimpeded, elemental *eros;* intense, chaotic, and cruel; the primitive, premoral, precultural condition of man and the world. If that force vindicates Medea as against Jason, her ardor as against his icy self-interest, it is only because her *eros* is elemental and therefore invincible. But she is vindicated only vis-à-vis Jason; and she is not *justified* at all. Of justification there can be no question here, not only because *eros* is, like any elemental necessity, amoral and therefore unjustifiable, but also because Euripides clearly believes the loss of *sophia* to be a tragic defeat for man and human culture.

In the agon of Jason and Medea, passion, vengeance, and self-interest expel *sophia.* That *agon,* as we have seen, stands for the Peloponnesian War—the war which Euripides, like Thucydides, feared would expel *sophia* from civilized cities, thereby barbarizing and brutalizing human behavior. At any time, in both individuals and cities, *sophia* is a delicate and precarious virtue; if anywhere in the Hellenic world, *sophia* flourished in Athens, but even there it bloomed precariously (how precariously the plague which overtook the city in the following year proved). And with the coming of Medea to Athens, Euripides seems to imply, comes the spirit of vengeance and passion, endangering *sophia,* that *sophia* whose creation and growth made Athens, in Thucydides' phrase, "the education of Hellas." For Hellas and humanity a new and terrible day dawns at the close of the *Medea.*

In sum, the Greeks possessed a recognizable and developed form of what we should not scruple to call a classical theater of ideas. And there, in substance, my argument rests. Whatever its critical shortcomings may be, its historical basis is, I think, sufficiently secure. If, historically, the theater of ideas tends to occur in times of severe cultural crisis, then we may properly expect it in late-fifth-century Athens, for of all the cultural crises of Hellenism, the late-fifth-century crisis was by far the most profound. Among its casualties are classical tragedy and comedy; the old mythical cosmology and the culture which it mirrored and sanctioned; the gods of the polis; the sense of community on which the polis was based, and therefore in a sense the polis itself. In short, the whole cloth of culture, fabric and design together.

In the fourth century Plato's attempt to repiece the old culture —to reconcile *physis* and *nomos,* myth and behavior, to reweave the moral community of the polis—was heroic but finally unsuccessful. Plato was a great conservative and a great revolutionary, but the Hellas he preserved was only preserved by being radically changed, in fact revolutionized. The old Greek culture—the culture to which the Western world most owes its being and to which it returns for life and freshness when Platonic Hellenism threatens to swamp it—died in the fifth century B.C., and it is this culture in its crisis of disintegration that Euripides records. If Euripides could no longer hold out the old heroic image of man, it is because he preferred to base his theater upon what he actually saw as the prime reality of his time: the new emerging human psyche, tested and defined by crisis, and the apparently uncontrollable chaos of human behavior and therefore the turbulence which any viable culture must know how to contain, but without repressing.

Put it this way. The complex knowledge and experience about

politics and culture so evident in *Hecuba* or the *Bacchae* look forward to Plato and also explain Plato's response to the same crisis. Both men share the conviction that war and greed for power have corrupted culture or deranged it; both are convinced that chaotic human nature, as revealed by crisis, cannot be controlled within the framework of existing culture. But Euripides' liberating perception has become Plato's restrictive premise. For Euripides any new cultural order must somehow contain what is uncontrollable in behavior; the failure to allow for turbulence, the failure to democratize its ethics, was what had made the old culture so susceptible to crisis. The Athenian democracy after Pericles could no more make do on aristocratic *sophrosunē* than industrial England could run on knightly chivalry. The solution, however, was not to reorganize society to operate on *sophrosunē* and the old aristocratic ethos but to revise *sophia* and *sophrosunē* in terms of a more democratic view of human nature. It is for this reason that in the *Bacchae* Pentheus' inability to control his inward turmoil is matched by his incompetence to control the public situation. He is an emblem of his age, attempting out of his ignorance of himself and his culture to cope with chaos by means of an inadequate or corrupted aristocratic *sophrosunē*. For whatever the solution to Dionysiac chaos may be, it is not repression, but perhaps a more responsibly Dionysiac (that is to say, liberated and liberating) society. The new polis may not be quite "polymorphously perverse," but it will at least be free, disciplined by experience of inward and outward chaos to a larger self-mastery.

For Plato the ideal polis can only be based upon a coercion that looks like consent. And it is therefore subject to the fate of

Euripides' Pentheus, the terrible revenge which *physis* takes upon a *nomos* that cannot enlarge itself to a true human order. In short, the culture envisaged by Plato rests ultimately upon suppression of the natural, and is to that degree profoundly pessimistic and anti-Hellenic. Euripides' specifications for culture rest upon an extremely realistic judgment of human nature and its potentialities for disorder; but because what is chaotic is seen as the thrust of life itself, as something *below* (or *beyond*) good or evil, morally neutral, culture is always a project for hope, for free order, for the creation of new institutions in which man's society will not be in conflict with his nature. The Athens which Euripides had so triumphantly hailed in the great choral ode of the *Medea* may have betrayed what it stood for, but the creative fusion between the passions (*erotes*) and the civilized and artistic skills (the large sense of *sophia*, nearly synonymous with "culture") which produced *arete—here*, however transient, was a paradigm of ideal social order, the polis which made man's fulfillment possible.

That Euripides is an innovator is, of course, not an altogether new idea; Werner Jaeger's word for him is, flatly, revolutionary. But those who regard Euripides as an innovator or a revolutionary rarely see in him much more than a theatrical sophist or the inventor of a realistic and psychological tragedy. So far as I know, nobody has seriously proposed what I am proposing here: that Euripides' theater is no less revolutionary than his ideas, and that these ideas are implicitly expressed in the assumptions of his theater and his dramatic hypotheses. In short, that his theater *is* his ideas; that his radical critique of crisis in culture is not just

Sophoclean tragedy turned topical and sophistic, but a wholly new theater, uneasily based upon the forms and conventions of the old. That is, not tragedy at all, but a critical drama related to Aeschylus and Sophocles in much the same way that Hebbel's theater was, at least in theory, related to Schiller's.[6] And for this very reason, I suppose, the argument will be discounted: Why, it will be objected, has a point like this been somehow missed for twenty-five hundred years?

To this question it is possible to make a great many answers. For one thing, the identification of the theater of ideas is of very recent date, even among critics of the theater. For another, classicists have traditionally been—as they remain—hostile or indifferent to literary criticism. For this reason they have very rarely asked the kind of question which might have led them to a literary answer. Instead of giving the dramatist the customary benefit of the doubt, they have assumed that a hostile tradition was generally sound and that Euripides was an interesting aber-

[6] A comparison I owe to Eric Bentley's *The Playwright as Thinker* (New York, 1955), p. 27. Hebbel described his new theater in this way: "At its every step there throngs around it a world of views and relations, which point both backwards and forwards, and all of which must be carried along; the life-forces cross and destroy one another, the thread of thought snaps in two before it is spun out, the emotion shifts, the very words gain their independence and reveal hidden meaning, annulling the ordinary one, for each is a die marked on more than one face. Here the chaff of little sentences, adding bit to bit and fiber to fiber, would serve the purpose ill. It is a question of presenting conditions in their organic totality. . . . Unevenness of rhythm, complication and confusion of periods, contradiction in the figures are elevated to effective and indispensable rhetorical means."

ration but finally too realistic, irreverent and vulgar to fill the bill as a bona fide classic. With deplorable regularity scholars have insisted that it was Euripides' fate to be an imitator or higher parodist of his predecessors, and then, just as regularly, have condemned him for bungling the job. I doubt, in fact, that the history of literature can show a more pathological chapter. Surely no great dramatist of the world has ever received less benefit of the critical doubt or been more consistently patronized; a fourth-rate Broadway hack will normally demand, and get, more courtesy from critics than Euripides has received from six centuries of scholarship. Even when he is praised by comparison with other dramatists, the comparison is inevitably patronizing. We do not honor our greatest classics by asserting their modernity; if classicists and critics compare Euripides to Ibsen, this is more to Ibsen's credit than to Euripides'—though this is *not* the assumption. We pay no honor to Shakespeare when we compliment him on his modernity: we merely reveal the true proportions of our contempt for the classics. Having said that, I can now say without being misunderstood: the theater of Brecht and of Sartre, and even the Theater of the Absurd, are in many ways remarkably like the theater of Euripides.

In any traditional perspective, Euripidean theater is complex and uncomfortably strange, almost exasperating to a taste founded on Aeschylus and Sophocles. Its premises, as we have seen, are unlike, and almost the inversion of, those of the traditional Greek theater. Typically it likes to conceal the truth beneath strata of irony because this is the look of truth: layered and elusive. For the same reason it presents its typical actions as problems and thereby involves the audience in a new relation, not as worshippers but as jurors who must resolve the problem by decision. But because the problem is usually incapable of outright resolution, is in fact tragic, the audience is compelled to forfeit the only luxury of making a decision—the luxury of *knowing* that one has decided wisely. Something—innocence, comfort, complacency—is always forfeited, or meant to be forfeited, by the audience of jurors. This suggests that the essential anagnorisis of Euripidean theater is not between one actor and another but between the audience and its own experience, as that experience is figured in the plays. Anagnorisis here is knowing moral choice, exercised on a problem which aims at mimicking the quandary of a culture. As such, it is a pattern of the way in which the psyche is made whole again, and the hope of a culture.

It is thus a difficult theater, and difficulty in literature, as opposed to textual difficulty or a doubtful manuscript reading, has never quickened the pulses of classical scholars. Indeed, the commonest scholarly response to the suggestion of a complex critical reading is that no classical writer could ever have been so unclear as not to be immediately transparent. If he was unclear or unusually complex or at all contorted, he was clearly unclassical; to such a degree has Winckelmann's criterion of "noble simplicity" seized the imagination of classical scholars. To those who believe that Euripides could not possibly have meant more than the little they are willing to understand, there is no adequate reply. But if it is true that critics who interpret great dramatists often seek to involve themselves in the dramatist's greatness, those who deny the dramatist any ideas but their own clearly involve the dramatist in their own dullness. John Finley's words to those who charge that more is read into Thucydides' speeches than the average Athenian citizen could have understood, are appropriate:

> It might be replied that the mass of the people could not have followed speeches of so general a character, but to make such an objection is to misunderstand the mind of the fifth century, indeed of any great period. The plays of Shakespeare and the sermons of early Protestantism give proof enough of the capacity assumed in an ordinary audience or congregation. It could be argued that any era which offers the ordinary man vast horizons of opportunity demands and receives from him a fresh comprehension proportionate to his fresh self-respect. Attic tragedy, even the philosophical and political subjects treated by Aristophanes, cannot be explained on any other assumption.[7]

As for Euripides, if I am right in assuming that his subject was nothing less than the life of Greek and Athenian culture, respect for the intelligence and good faith of the ordinary audience *must* be forthcoming, since it is the premise of culture itself. If Euripides for the most part failed to win the understanding of his audience, as I think he did, the fact does not disprove the intent. It is, I think, not sufficiently recognized that the very scholars who object that literary criticism means importing modern prejudices into an ancient text are themselves usually the worst offenders. Utterly unconsciously they take for granted all the cramping prejudices which a culture like ours can confer upon an uncritical man, and confer them in turn upon antiquity. "The

[7] John H. Finley, Jr., *Thucydides.* (Cambridge, Mass., 1947), pp. 64–65.

classicist's attitude toward the ancient world," wrote Nietzsche, "is either apologetic or derives from the notion that what our age values highly can also be found in antiquity. The right starting-point is the opposite, i.e., to start from the perception of modern absurdity and to look backward from that viewpoint—and many things regarded as offensive in the ancient world will appear as profound necessities. We must make it clear to ourselves that we are acting absurdly when we justify or beautify antiquity: who are *we*?"

Among literary men and critics of literature, as opposed to scholars, it might be assumed that a Greek theater of ideas would find favor, if only as a sanction and precedent for the new intellectual theater. But I suspect that this is not the case, precisely because contemporary critics are so stubbornly and unreasonably convinced that the entire Greek theater from Aeschylus to Euripides is firmly ritualistic. In saying this, I am thinking of the fact that the modern poetic theater, in searching for anti-naturalistic models, turned significantly to Greek drama. What interested contemporaries in Greek drama was, of course, the belief that they would find in it those features—ritual, stylization, gesture, a sacramental sense of life and community—which promised release from the restrictions of the naturalistic theater. They were confirmed in this by the literary vogue of anthropology, and the apparent success of the so-called Cambridge school, especially Francis Cornford and Jane Harrison. But the strongest argument for the ritual view of Greek drama came, I think, from the inability of the classicists themselves to give any substantial meaning to Greek drama. Thus literary men, always a little nervous when confronted with a Greek text and seldom inclined to quarrel with scholarship, eagerly accepted a scholarly view of the Greek plays that at least had the merit of making them mean *something* and which also suited their own theatrical programs. Ritual for them was a "find." For Greek drama it was, as I have tried to show elsewhere, an unqualified disaster.

But because its basis is "need," ritual interpretation is particularly insidious. My own objections to it are threefold; first, the belief that developed tragedy still bears the visible structural and esthetic effects of its origin is a clear case of the genetic fallacy; second, there is so little evidence for it in extant tragedy that its own originator, Gilbert Murray, recanted it; and third, it is really Cornford's argument for comedy—a far sounder argument in view of comedy's late nationalization—that gives it cogency. My critical objection to the ritual approach is that it tends to diminish rather than enhance the literary value of the plays; in short, it tends to make priests of tragedians and worshippers of audiences. This is not, of course, to deny the religious importance of the Greek tragedian or his religious concern. But it is to deny that his subject was prescribed, his treatment wholly conventional or stylized, and his thought unimportant or unadventurous. Whatever value the ritual approach may have for Aeschylus or Sophocles (and I think the value is small), its application has obscured even further the nature and originality of the Euripidean theater of ideas, since it is precisely discursive, *critical* thought, the complex dialectic of Euripidean drama, that ritualist interpretation regularly suppresses. Thus the only result of the ritual criticism of Greek drama has been, in my opinion, a further falsification.

But the essential, the crucial reason for our misunderstanding of Greek drama in general, and Euripidean theater in particular, is one which classicists and literary men alike share with the whole modern world. And this is our special cultural need of the classics, our own crucial myth of classical culture. A tradition is, after all, like love; we "crystallize" it, endow it with the perfections it must have in order to justify our need and our love. And classical Greek culture has for some time stood in relation to modern culture as a measure of our own chaos—a cultural Eden by which we measure our fall from grace and innocence. Thus we view the Greeks with the same envious and needful wonder that Nietzsche and Thomas Mann reserved for Goethe—that integrated soul—and which Euripides' age felt for the age of Aeschylus. To our modern dissonance, the Greeks play the role of old tonality, the abiding image of a great humanity. They are our lost power; lost wholeness; the pure *presence* and certainty of reality our culture has lost.

Against a need like this and a myth like this, argument may be futile. But we should not, I think, be allowed to mythologize unawares. If we first deprive classical culture of its true turbulence in order to make ourselves a myth of what we have lost, and then hedge that myth with false ritual, we are depriving ourselves of that community of interest and danger that makes the twentieth century true kin to the Greeks. We deprive ourselves, in short, of access to what the past can teach us in order to take only what we want. And that is a cultural loss of the first magnitude.

❦

# From Myth to Ideas—and Back

My title represents, as so many English Institute titles do, the aspirations of February rather than the achievements of September. The impulses associated with St. Valentine's Day fade at the approach of the autumnal equinox.

My chief purpose as director of the 1962 conference was to show that the drama of ideas can claim a far longer lineage than most critics have assigned to it. The term "drama of ideas" may date from no earlier than the last quarter of the nineteenth century, though Eric Bentley traces the concept back as far as Lessing. The thing itself, however, as I hope Mr. Arrowsmith's paper has already convinced you, is almost coeval with the first mature Western drama, that of the Greeks.

My original hope for my own paper was that it would fill the gap between the Age of Pericles and the Age of Khrushchev with a series of Viconian cycles. As the ritual of Dionysus at Athens led to mythic drama, which in turn led to the Euripidean drama of ideas, so I thought that Christian ritual could be shown to lead to the mythic drama of the mystery plays and thence, inevitably, to drama of ideas once more, as represented by the morality plays. From there I could move to a fresh cycle in which the court ritual of the new absolute monarchies would lead, via the mythic drama of the court masques or the monarchist myth of Shakespeare's history plays, to the drama of ideas of the mature Shakespeare. In France, I could proceed from Corneille's myth of honor to Molière's drama of ideas. And who could tell what lesser cycles, what wheels within wheels, might not proliferate thereafter? For example, the mature work of Ibsen begins with inherited myth in *Peer Gynt,* passes through the phase of drama of ideas, and culminates in a new myth of Ibsen's own creation, *When We Dead Awaken.*

My cyclical theory of drama was a beautiful invention. It had only one drawback: it would not fit the facts. I prefer to say that the facts would not fit *it.* The life force is a poor philosopher and an even worse literary critic.

The first stumbling block to my theory arose right at the beginning, among the Greeks. If George Thomson is right, drama of ideas began with Aeschylus.[1] I am not referring to the *Persae,* the first extant play on a subject contemporary with its author, but to the third part of the *Oresteia,* the *Eumenides,* where the relative merits of tribal blood feud and civilized justice by an impartial court are examined. Perhaps even more disturbing to my thesis than Mr. Thomson's *Aeschylus and Athens* was Benjamin Hunningher's *The Origin of the Theater,*[2] which argues cogently against the view that drama was reborn out of Christian ritual; if the drama was in fact reborn in the Middle Ages instead of merely continuing the traditions of Roman mime, then it sprang, Mr. Hunningher maintains, from the same sort of pagan fertility ritual that engendered Greek drama in the first place. Furthermore, as I hope to show later, the morality play cannot be properly classified as a drama of ideas in the nineteenth-century meaning of the term.

[1] *Aeschylus and Athens,* 2d ed., (London, 1946).
[2] New York, 1961.

Even if I substitute the term "orthodoxy" or "orthodox world view" for "myth" in my title, I run into difficulties. At least twice in the history of British drama one finds a series of developments which can be schematized as a sort of Hegelian dialectic, but the schematization is very imperfect. To say that medieval drama provides the thesis, Marlowe's "Machiavellian" drama the antithesis, and Shakespeare's mature work the synthesis makes a neat pattern, but it ignores two facts: medieval drama had been moribund for at least a century before Marlowe, and the Reformation had occurred in the interim. E. M. W. Tillyard's *The Elizabethan World Picture* [3] has taught us all that the Middle Ages were an unconscionable time a-dying, but one need only take another look at Shakespeare to realize that Mr. Tillyard has not given us the whole picture; in correcting a distorted view, he has made us swing too far in the other direction and forget the Renaissance and Reformation elements in the Elizabethan picture: the persecuting Protestant in Spenser's make-up and the deists and atheists who belonged to Raleigh's circle.

I find it truer to say that before the new synthesis of medieval, Renaissance, and Protestant thought had found adequate expression in the drama a full-fledged antiorthodoxy sprang up in the work of Marlowe. The struggles of orthodoxy to counter this begot another kind of synthesis which often takes the form of drama of ideas. The closing of the theaters during the Civil War swept away this synthesis, and when the theaters reopened under Charles II antiorthodoxy, in comedy at least, was dominant once more. Tentative signs of a new synthesis began to show themselves in the work of Farquhar, but he died too soon; shortly

[3] London, 1943.

afterwards a complacent, antiintellectual version of orthodoxy reestablished itself.

The preceding points will be discussed in more detail in the body of this paper, which deals chiefly with British drama from Marlowe to Shaw and French drama from Molière to Beaumarchais. Ibsen, whose translated works I swallowed whole in my youth with the exception of *Emperor and Galilaean,* will serve as a permanent touchstone on which to test the authenticity of alleged examples of drama of ideas.

It is time to offer a tentative definition of drama of ideas. As Eric Bentley writes: "Idea is a vague concept. In one sense there are ideas in all words and therefore in all drama." However, so long as the dramatist and his contemporary audience share the same world view, we shall find very little comment on his ideas as such, and most of that comment can be summed up in the phrase "How true!" Mr. Bentley continues: "In a drama of ideas . . . the ideas are questioned, and it is by the questioning, and could only be by the questioning, that the ideas become dramatic, for never is there drama without conflict." [4] In other words, only when an audience finds its cherished orthodoxy questioned does it take note, often in a tone of indignation, that a dramatist is dealing in ideas. Mr. Bentley's definition is a more general statement of Shaw's position in *The Quintessence of Ibsenism:*

In the new plays, the drama arises through a conflict of unsettled ideals rather than through vulgar attachments, rapacities, generosities, resentments, ambitions, misunderstandings, oddities and so forth as to which no moral question is raised. The

[4] *The Playwright As Thinker* (New York, 1955), p. 51.

conflict is not between clear right and wrong: the villain is as
conscientious as the hero, if not more so: in fact, the question
which makes the play interesting (when it *is* interesting) is
which is the villain and which the hero.[5]

Shaw's formulation is much more penetrating than Mr. Bentley's.
The drama of ideas ought really to be called the drama of ideals,
for it presents not one isolated idea pitted against another but a
conflict of opposing world views or ideologies. Note Shaw's insistence that "the conflict is not between clear right and wrong";
in consequence, the dramatist may feel so ambivalent about both
sides of a particular issue that he refuses to permit either to score
a clear victory. A common criticism leveled against drama of
ideas alleges that it oversimplifies issues and comes to pat conclusions. This criticism is only justified where poor dramatists have
attempted this difficult genre and failed dismally. True drama of
ideas is so riddled with ambiguity that even a sophisticated
audience may be left wondering not only which is the hero and
which the villain but which is the victor and which the van-
quished. These are precisely the questions which a drama of
orthodoxy cannot afford to leave in doubt. Milton can safely
assign the best speech in his masque to Comus, but he cannot
allow him to win the argument with the Lady, although if he
were writing a tragedy instead of a masque he might allow
Comus to overcome her chastity by force.

Shaw might have added that in orthodox drama not only the
audience but the villain himself usually know who the villain is,
because both villain and hero share the same conceptions of right

[5] *Major Critical Essays* (London, 1932), p. 139.

and wrong. We need not think in terms of anything so crude as Richard III's assertion that he is "determined to prove a villain." Or need we? When one reflects upon it, the pagan demigod Comus' assertion " 'Tis only daylight that makes sin" seems almost as incongruous. What does he know or care about sin?

In the light of Shaw's rigorous definition, it is easy to see why the morality play cannot be described as a drama of ideas: it is too one-sided. Not only do we know who the villain is and who the victor is, but we know before the play starts just who the victor *must* be. *Everyman* can be considered a special case, since the conflict is not between good and evil so much as between knowledge and ignorance. At each stage of his journey toward the grave, Everyman has to part with some cherished illusion. He also has to part with various cherished companions, but in only one instance, that of Fellowship, does the parting really constitute a betrayal. The other separations are an inevitable part of the human condition, and no blame attaches to those involved in them. The unique appeal of *Everyman* for recent generations is perhaps due to the points it has in common with the drama of ideas, but at best this play is not very dramatic.

One of the greatest misconceptions about Ibsen held by those who have not seen or read his social dramas is that he makes a frontal assault on the weaknesses of bourgeois society or, alternatively, sets up an ideal of free love from the moment the curtain rises. Nothing, of course, could be farther from the truth. Yet it is hard to blame those ignorant of Ibsen for taking this view when nineteenth-century London drama critics who *had* seen the plays took exactly the same attitude. All that is necessary to refute them is a reading of the opening pages of *A Doll's House,* which

present a white-collar idyl straight from today's women's maga-
zines: hubby just promoted to an executive position, attractive
wife, three kids, endearments flying about, cosy private jokes.
Underneath, of course, lies the abyss. But if the Helmers' marriage
were in fact an ideal one, the pillars of society would have been
insane not to applaud Ibsen for making marriage so attractive.
This technique of bending over backwards to be fair to what is
going to be questioned apparently infuriated the critics, who
felt they had been "had." Perhaps a frontal attack would have
aroused less indignation. So, at any rate, a consideration of some
of Marlowe's plays and of Restoration comedy in general may
lead us to think.

In these works all the orthodox ideals are stood on their heads.
The negation of official doctrine in both church and state is en-
throned upon the stage and shows little mercy to more conventional ideals. The one-sidedness of these plays makes me question
their right to be considered any closer to the drama of ideas than
the morality plays, even though they are one-sided on the opposite,
unorthodox side. Nothing even remotely resembling them would
have been tolerated on the French stage at that time. Does this
prove that English audiences were really so much more broad-
minded than their foreign contemporaries or than their own
descendants? Or must we think that these audiences were too
unphilosophical to recognize the plays' transvaluation of values?
Whatever the reason, Marlowe held the stage uninterruptedly for
fifty years and Restoration comedy held it for at least thirty.

It will be said that I am taking too simple-minded a view of
Restoration comedy, but it is always a shock to reread Wycherley's
*The Country Wife,* admittedly the extreme example of the genre.

It is all very well to say that Restoration comedy contains an implicit norm against which antisocial behavior is measured. For instance, the statement that "men are now more ashamed to be seen with [their wives] in public than with a wench" only becomes humorous or satirical when contrasted with the normal assumption that men should be proud to be seen with their wives, or at least ashamed to be seen with their wenches. But the explicit norms of most of the characters in the play are so antisocial that it seems futile to measure their actions by traditional moral standards; in that case, what happens to the humor and the satire? In cold print, away from the glamour of the stage, one finds in *The Country Wife* only a group of thoroughly unattractive people all trying to get the better of one another and disguising their fraud and malice as love and wit. (The fact that critics *read* plays while audiences only see them may explain why Restoration comedy, in the words of Norman N. Holland: "has almost always been the darling of audiences, but a strumpet to critics.")[6]

Unless I greatly misunderstand him, Mr. Holland is but one of several contemporary critics—all strumpetless, of course—who would like us to accept Restoration comedy as a special case of the drama of ideas. I should like to explain in a little more detail why I must reject their offer. Let me use *The Country Wife* to illustrate what I mean by the one-sidedness of Restoration comedy—the absence of a fair confrontation of ideals.

The life of Horner does represent an ideal, after all. He possesses to a supreme degree the two supreme satisfactions of a Restoration rake: the knowledge that he is wittier (we should

[6] *The First Modern Comedies* (Cambridge, Mass., 1959), p. 3.

now say "cleverer" or "more cunning") than those around him
and the opportunity to enjoy complete sexual promiscuity to the
limit of his physical powers. Such success is as imaginary and
ideal in its own way as the contrary picture of a loving, intelligent, and faithful husband married to a loving, intelligent, and
faithful wife and raising a large, happy family of legitimate children. The achievement of the latter ideal is certainly no more
improbable than becoming a successful Horner. But we are never
given a chance to choose the more orthodox ideal, which is dismissed from the start as an impossibility. Pinchwife or Jasper
Fidget is the nearest approximation to the ideal husband permitted by Wycherley—namely, a complacent or a grudging
cuckold. On the other hand, Wycherley does play fair in remind-
ing us that many are called, but few are chosen, to fill the role
of a Horner. It could be one's fate to end as a Sparkish.

Harcourt is a problem. Is he a failed Horner or will he become
a slightly less undignified Pinchwife? Certainly his future wife,
Alithea (*Aletheia,* "Truth"?), is intelligent, as Mrs. Pinchwife
is not, but will she be faithful? Her maid thinks so. Will Harcourt be faithful? The signs point to the contrary. The circumstances of their wooing make us dubious about their married
life, which will not begin until the play is over. Harcourt's slick
courtship of Alithea under the very eyes of Sparkish, her fiancé,
and her readiness to jilt the idiotic Sparkish once she finds him
capable of jealousy cannot be described as good omens.

In just one respect *The Country Wife* fits Shaw's definition of
the drama of ideas very aptly. Which is the villain of the play and
which the hero? From the Victorian standpoint, Horner seems the

only possible candidate for the villain, but, as we have already seen, he looks much more plausible as the hero. Similarly, Mrs. Pinchwife (the title role) seems cut out for the heroine, whatever the partisans of Alithea may say; yet this country wife would appear a villainess to Victorian eyes. Mrs. Pinchwife has the directness of a natural force and attains her end in spite of all the obstacles, whereas Alithea, rather than choose a line of conduct for herself, merely reacts to her suitors' behavior.

In his next and last play, *The Plain Dealer,* Wycherley swung violently around to the opposite extreme and denounced the chicanery of his society from an essentially orthodox moral standpoint. It is only when the Restoration impulse is dying that Farquhar, in the last act of his last play (*The Beaux' Stratagem*), produces a true equivalent of nineteenth-century drama of ideas. The characters in Restoration comedy have always been addicted to discussions of matrimony as an institution, but their comments are purely destructive. In contrast, the discussions of marriage conducted by Sir Charles Freeman, Squire Sullen, and Mrs. Sullen in *The Beaux' Stratagem* reach a moderately constructive solution: if a marriage is hopelessly unsatisfactory to both parties, they should obtain a divorce and try again. Some of the dialogue has a remarkably Shavian ring; for example, Freeman's retort to Boniface: "You and your wife, Mr. Guts, may be one flesh, because ye are nothing else; but rational creatures have minds that must be united." Mrs. Sullen comments with insight and feeling upon the narrow legal grounds for divorce: "Can a jury sum up the endless aversions that are rooted in our souls, or can a bench give judgment upon antipathies?" A brisk and brilliant

exchange of repartee between the Squire and his wife in the final
scene proves that their marriage has utterly failed to meet the
expectations of either party, and they agree to seek a divorce.

Unfortunately, Farquhar died within weeks after completing
this play, at the age of twenty-nine. No successor arose to carry
on his attempt at a synthesis between the old ideas and the new.
With the notable exception of the antiorthodox *The Beggar's
Opera*, the rest of eighteenth-century British drama provides a
cosy reaffirmation of traditional values, replete with brainy villains
and stupid heroes, typified by Joseph and Charles Surface in
*The School for Scandal*.

Restoration antiorthodoxy may have been more subtle than I
am prepared to admit, but surely nothing could be less subtle
than Marlowe's attack on orthodoxy in *Tamburlaine, Part I*, or in
*The Jew of Malta*. The consensus of Marlowe scholarship insists
that the first part of *Tamburlaine* is complete in itself and was
intended to be so. In it, Tamburlaine advances from victory to
cruel victory without any consciousness of sin on either his own
or his author's part. Even when Tamburlaine succumbs to death
in *Part II*, there is no hint that he has been guilty of the Christian
sin of pride or the Greek one of *hubris*. Paul H. Kocher is surely
justified in saying of Tamburlaine's famous speech about "the
sweet fruition of an earthly crown" that Marlowe's character
"here speaks like a prior incarnation of Nietzsche." [7]

Christian values are not referred to at all in *Tamburlaine*, but
Mr. Kocher's phrase about Marlowe's "struggle with Christianity"
finds explicit support in *The Jew of Malta*. For me, as for Mr.

[7] *Christopher Marlowe: A Study of his Thought, Learning, and Character*
(New York, 1962), p. 72.

Kocher, the play contains no ambiguity: Barabas is the hero. The ambiguity lies in the reception of the play by the Elizabethan popular audience, who would assume that a Jew must be a villain. F. P. Wilson tells us that the play was a particular favorite with the utterly unsophisticated Shrovetide audiences.[8] The daring prologue spoken by Machiavel might alert the avant-garde, but since Machiavelli was only a bogeyman to the popular audience the fact that he approved of Barabas would be one more argument against the Jew.

Although *The Jew of Malta* permits some confrontation of Christianity with extreme individualism—not with Judaism, for Barabas is not a believing Jew—the case is prejudged, for Christian practice at its worst, rather than Christian principle, is used as the standard. Christians, in Barabas' view, are all hypocrites, and the Christian characters in the play all bear out his opinion:

Who hateth me but for my happiness?
Or who is honour'd now but for his wealth?
Rather had I, a Jew, be hated thus,
Than pitied in a Christian poverty;
For I can see no fruits in all their faith,
But malice, falsehood, and excessive pride,
Which methinks fits not their profession.

Only the most dubious of Christian principles are obeyed, and these alone Barabas finds worthy of imitation:

It's no sin to deceive a Christian;
For they themselves hold it a principle,

[8] *Marlowe and the Early Shakespeare* (Oxford, 1953), p. 67.

Faith is not to be held with heretics:
But all are heretics that are not Jews.

After much more of this sort of criticism from Barabas and many
instances of greed and deceit on the part of the two friars in the
play, it hardly seems important that Barabas should finally over-
reach himself and be defeated by the nominally Christian Ferneze,
who had dealt so unjustly with him in the early stages of the
action. I find it very strange that Thomas Heywood, whose own
plays show a fairly conventional and even sentimental morality,
should have made it his business to publish *The Jew of Malta,*
"composed by so worthy an author as Master Marlowe," [9] in the
reign of Charles the Martyr.

*Dr. Faustus* is the only play by Marlowe that, because of the im-
partiality with which it treats the conflict between the Christian
ideal and that of extreme individualism, deserves to be classed as
a true drama of ideas. Otherwise, the orthodox Shakespeare gives
us a far closer approximation to drama of ideas than the revolutionary Marlowe. Shakespeare lacked the scholarship of a Donne
or a Marlowe, but he was fully aware that "new Philosophy calls
all in doubt." [10] The revolution in science meant little to him, but
the "new realism" in politics and morality typified by Machiavelli
concerned him greatly. In play after play he confronted the new
realism with the old idealism and let them fight it out on sur-
prisingly level terms. The attempt of modern historicism to see
his plays as the Elizabethans saw them has had the unexpected

[9] Christopher Marlowe, *Plays* (London, 1909), p. 159.
[10] John Donne, "An Anatomie of the World: The First Anniversary."

effect of controverting Shaw, who by and large condemned Shakespeare for not being a dramatist of ideas.

Take *King Lear*. Our modern reading of it as in part an examination of what is meant by "nature" and "natural" classes *King Lear* with numerous plays by Shaw and Ibsen which raise the question of whether it is natural for children to love and honor their parents. Shakespeare's answer seems to be that it is not; parents, unless they happen to be very lucky, have to earn their children's love and respect. On the other hand, Shakespeare drives home the orthodox point that, unless children do love and respect their parents, society as he knows it will disintegrate, without any assurance that a better form of society may come in its place.

Our modern interpretation of the histories points to a similar lesson. Shakespeare does not share the idealist illusion that a legitimate king must be a competent administrator or even a just man. On the other hand, for all the glamour shed over the King in *Henry V*, we are not allowed to forget that his own security and that of his kingdom are always threatened by his shaky status as the son of a usurper.

Often, as we know, the subversive ideas are relegated to the comic plot, where they cannot compete on equal terms with the orthodox views that share the prestige of the heroic characters. Falstaff's critique of honor and his gleeful acceptance of war as offering a better cloak for swindling than does peace can be taken humorously and/or seriously according to taste. But is *Troilus and Cressida*, that favorite of Shaw's, really any more of an antiwar play than *Henry IV, Part I?* Achilles' homosexuality and cowardice, Menelaus' oft-cited cuckoldry, and the stupidity of Ajax cannot altogether overshadow the bravery and nobility of Hector. As for Thersites, his position is exactly analogous to Falstaff's; each is a comic role, but Falstaff was presumably written for Will Kempe and Thersites for Robert Armin.

Altogether too much fuss has been made about Shakespeare's "problem comedies"—mainly at Shaw's instigation, I may remind you. Recall, for instance, the passage in the preface to *Plays Unpleasant* where he says that Shakespeare "has left us no intellectually coherent drama, and could not afford to pursue a genuinely scientific method in his studies of character and society, though in such unpopular plays as All's Well, Measure for Measure, and Troilus and Cressida, we find him ready and willing to start at the twentieth century if the seventeenth would only let him." [11] In my opinion we should pay more attention to the problem tragedies and the problem histories than to the problem comedies. Since 1913, when Shaw made his last revisions of *The Quintessence of Ibsenism,* scholarship has done much to support his admission that "anyhow . . . Shakespeare survives by what he has in common with Ibsen, and not by what he has in common with Webster and the rest."[12]

It is very instructive to compare French drama of the seventeenth and eighteenth centuries with English drama of the same period. One might assume that the French intellectual tradition, with its readiness to think in abstract terms and to push a train of thought to its logical limit, would be much more favorable to drama of ideas than the English tradition. Such a view, however,

[11] *Prefaces* (London, 1934), p. 692.
[12] *Major Critical Essays,* p. 142.

would fundamentally misunderstand the nature of the drama of ideas. The theater cannot deal successfully in abstractions, even personified abstractions, as the morality plays and the German Expressionist drama have pretty conclusively demonstrated. The great problem for the dramatist of ideas lies in the drama rather than in the ideas. If he cannot create interesting characters who embody in their own conflicts the conflicts of ideas or ideals, his work will satisfy neither actors nor audiences. Furthermore, the supreme achievement in the drama of ideas, as in the more conventional drama, is the creation of characters who embody both sides of a conflict within a single personality. Mrs. Alving in *Ghosts,* torn between the old morality and the new, represents a far greater theatrical triumph than Nora in *A Doll's House,* who becomes almost exclusively a representative of the new morality, while her husband makes a weak and disappointing representative of the old. The tension at the end of *A Doll's House* used to be generated by the audience's prejudice against the views expressed by Nora; now that most people take Nora's side, the last act has lost much of its power. The tension at the end of *Ghosts,* tension *within* Mrs. Alving which communicates itself to the audience, still remains almost unbearable.

Those who expect much mature drama of ideas in seventeenth- and eighteenth-century France are at fault for another reason too. They are forgetting history. No other branch of literature is so much at the mercy of social and political forces as the drama. Here, if anywhere, Marxist criticism comes into its own. Has it ever occurred to anyone to ask why the Irish, who have so dominated the English-speaking theater as dramatists and to a considerable degree as performers also, never developed a Gaelic-

speaking theater? The answer is very simple: there has never
been a Gaelic-speaking city, a Gaelic polis. Up to the collapse of
Gaelic civilization around the year 1600, what towns and cities
there were in Ireland had been founded and were dominated by
Norse, Norman, or English invaders. Seventeenth- and eighteenth-century France was under the control of absolute monarchy
and the Roman Catholic Church, whereas England was slowly—
too slowly— developing a mutually tolerant plurality of Protestant sects and a constitutional monarchy. The English theaters
could be completely suppressed, as they were under the Common-
wealth, but freedom of speech and of the press was relatively
far more widespread in England during this period than it was in
France. Voltaire's *Lettres philosophiques* show quite clearly that
in moving from France to England he found that he had also
traveled from the seventeenth century to the eighteenth. Even
after the Licensing Act of 1737 the English theater was still freer
than its French counterpart.

Censorship of the theater explains why Voltaire's plays are so
conventional, though their conventionality does not entirely explain their tediousness. Any of his other work that was likely
to be censored could be published in Amsterdam, say, and
smuggled into France, but what was the point of writing French
plays that could not be performed in Paris? Voltaire's plays may
in fact be less tedious than they appear; unfortunately, one tries
to read them with one's head full of *Candide;* the unconven-
tionality of that work emphasizes the conventionality of the plays
to an unbearable degree.

I am not saying that in Voltaire we lost a great dramatist of
ideas; for one thing, he lacked the power to create highly in-

dividual characters: Candide, Pangloss, and the rest are two-dimensional. Our great loss, as I see it, consists of the plays that Diderot might have written. Even as it was, he became one of the pioneers of the "serious" middle-class play—neither tragedy nor comedy.

In a sense, *Le Père de famille* can be called a drama of ideas, and even one of a rather subtle kind. Diderot's father of a family is no authoritarian, in spite of his son's angry cry that there are no fathers, only tyrants. On the contrary, M. d'Orbesson is a Rousseauistic liberal who has raised and educated his son personally without the aid of nursemaids or tutors. As a result, when the son appears to be set on wrecking his own future, the father is made far more unhappy than any domestic tyrant could possibly become. Fortunately, M. d'Orbesson refuses to exert his authority arbitrarily, realizing that this would only alienate his son's affection and guarantee his own permanent unhappiness.

Regrettably, the whole logic of the play as a drama of ideas is shattered by the revelation that the penniless unknown whom the son wants to marry is a relative of his mother. This is the kind of contrived happy ending that infuriated Shaw when it occurred in Shakespeare. We can only be thankful that Diderot did not make Sophie an heiress as well as of eligible birth. The notion that a liberal idealist can create domestic unhappiness for himself would have appealed to the author of *The Wild Duck*. Diderot's espousal of bourgeois rather than aristocratic ideals does not entirely blind him to their flaws.

To guess at the master dramatist lost to us in Diderot, one must turn from *Le Père de famille* to *Le Neveu de Rameau,* a dialogue so subversive that Diderot may never have dreamed of publishing

it during his lifetime. Of course dialogue is not drama. Not even
the *Symposium,* for all its vivid characterization of Socrates and
Alcibiades, can be claimed as a forerunner of drama of ideas. For
drama it is not sufficient that characters should sit and talk about
their ideals: they must act in accordance with them. But Diderot
showed in several plays that he was capable of creating meaningful action, while in Rameau he created, or re-created, a character overflowing with vitality of speech and gesture, infinitely
more believable and interesting than any figure in his plays, and
similar to but far more complex than Shaw's Dubedat in *The
Doctor's Dilemma.*

*Le Neveu de Rameau* defies summary: viewed from one aspect
it is a confrontation of Diderot, representing the Age of Reason,
with Rameau, representing the Romantic Age of Excess that has
yet to arrive; from another aspect, Diderot seems the idealist and
Rameau the realist; from still another aspect the dialogue reads
like a confrontation of the superego with the id. If one explored
the riches of this vest-pocket encyclopedia long enough, one could
probably discover in it all the themes of Ibsen and Shaw.

Since Diderot did not write the plays he might have, we are
left with only one French dramatist of ideas in the two centuries
—Molière, of course. He is a subject almost as big as Shakespeare
and in some ways more confusing. Critics still cannot agree
whether Molière was a revolutionary or a conservative in morals
and theology, though the majority favor the latter view. This
ambiguity in itself proves his skill as a dramatist of ideas. Yet I
think he wrote at most three plays of ideas: *Le Tartuffe, Don
Juan,* and *Le Misanthrope.* The only possible fourth, *George*

*Dandin,* never really comes to grips with its subject, which is class distinction. No doubt the uproar over *Tartuffe* and the suppression of the play for five years quickly robbed Molière of any desire to handle ticklish subjects. The three plays belong to three successive years, 1664 to 1666, after which he began to play it safe.

A priori, and in view of the numerous denunciations of this vice which may be read in the Gospels, one would not have thought religious hypocrisy to be a particularly dangerous subject. But not even the introduction of the King's officer as *deus ex machina* and the personal approval of Louis XIV himself could save *Tartuffe* from temporary suppression. It is not the function of the drama of ideas to denounce what everybody disapproves of; some genuinely pious people clearly felt (and some still do feel) that Molière's play holds up to ridicule not only Tartuffe's hypocrisy but all conspicuous devotion, however genuine.

Actually, *Don Juan* is a far more dangerous play than *Tartuffe,* though naïve people accepted it more readily because Don Juan went to hell in the end. Tirso de Molina's whole conception of the Don's character has been radically altered by Molière. In *El Burlador de Sevilla,* Don Juan was a believer who mistakenly felt that he still had plenty of time left in which to repent. Molière's hero, however, is an avowed atheist who deliberately breaks just about all of the Ten Commandments and at first refuses to be hypocritical about his unbelief. I find him very hard to dislike. When a pious poor man refuses to commit a sin for money, Don Juan gives him the coin anyway "for the love of humanity."

Molière's version of Don Juan does not forfeit our sympathy until he becomes a hypocrite and pretends to his father that he has reformed. Prior to that point, he was as true to his unfaith as the poor man was to his faith. Actually, as we soon discover, Don Juan's conversion to hypocrisy is a further move in the *Tartuffe* controversy. In the longest, most brilliant speech of the play he explains to Sganarelle that hypocrisy is a fashionable vice and that fashionable vices pass for virtues; all men's other vices are subject to censure, and everyone has the right to attack them openly, but hypocrisy is a privileged vice. Hypocrites band together to support one another, and if Don Juan is exposed *toute la cabale* will spring to his defense. At last he has found the true means to do what he likes with impunity. As Sganarelle says, becoming a hypocrite was the only thing lacking to make the Don a complete scoundrel: "I believe that Heaven, which has put up with you so far, will not be able to endure this final horror." True to Sganarelle's prophecy, the statue of the Commander arrives almost immediately to drag Don Juan to hell. This ironic ending can hardly have afforded much comfort to the enemies of *Le Tartuffe*.

Of *Le Misanthrope*, as of *Hamlet*, no interpretation will ever be accepted as final. It seems to me that even if we write off Alceste as a neurotic, his denunciation of a society based on insincerity still remains valid.[18] Philinte is often assumed to be the true spokesman for Molière, but this *honnête homme* is assigned some rather ridiculous speeches; for example,

[18] See Martin Turnell's profound discussion of the play in *The Classical Moment* (London, 1947), pp. 90–120. Mr. Turnell is more inclined to regard Alceste as a neurotic than I am.

Si tous les coeurs étoient francs, justes et dociles,
La plupart des vertus nous seroient inutiles.

(If all hearts were frank, just and open to reason,
most of our virtues would be useless to us.)

One cannot blame Alceste for rudely cutting Philinte short. Most of us would be content to find a few of our numerous virtues useless under such circumstances. Éliante, who is just as intelligent and reasonable as Philinte, if not more so, says that the sincerity on which Alceste prides himself has something intrinsically noble and heroic about it. She wishes everybody were like him.

Surely the most intelligent evaluation of this play is to deny the victory to either side. If Alceste is guilty of absurdities, that does not make society any the less corrupt. If he is foolish enough to fall in love with the most inveterate coquette in Paris, at least he is not mad enough to marry her when she refuses to leave the city with him. His desire to seek some place off the beaten track, where one is free to be a man of honor, does not seem absurd or neurotic to me. If Philinte foolishly wishes to thwart this plan, that is just what one would expect from such a busybody. Alceste's great talents are not of a kind that will flower in society or wither in solitude.

Le Misanthrope is one of the purest examples of the drama of ideas, a member of that very small group of plays which tease the mind long after one has left the theater. In a seemingly casual, laughing way it poses unanswerable questions about the proper relationship between the exceptional individual and society.

Since I mentioned Beaumarchais earlier, I had better not ignore
him entirely, although I cannot take him seriously as a dramatist
of ideas. Of all the classics I read in my youth, *Le Mariage de
Figaro* was the most disappointing. However, in reading it I
conceived a great respect for the French: if this play could make
them start a revolution, what a flammable people they must be!
My more mature objection to the play has been precisely expressed by Jacques Barzun:

> The truth is that Figaro's ideas about society were hardly new,
> except on the stage, when they appeared there in 1784. Thanks
> to the "liberals" of a century before, to Montesquieu and
> Voltaire, to Diderot and the Encyclopedists, thanks above all
> to Rousseau's writings and personality, the enlightened aristoc-
> racy and high bourgeoisie of the eighteenth century were quite
> convinced that birth was worthless compared to talents, and
> that established authority cloaked incompetence and injustice.
> A theatrical audience could respond to Figaro's indignation
> because it seemed not so much subversive as appropriate.[14]

I would be the last person to say that the drama of ideas has to
deal with absolutely new ideas, but I must insist once again that
a play which tells its audience exactly what they want to hear
cannot claim a place in that category. By 1784 the French theater
was as far behind the times as the English theater was to be a
century later. As Shaw said of the Victorian period, one was more
likely to encounter advanced ideas in a church than on the stage.

[14] Robert Lowell and Jacques Barzun, *Phaedra and Figaro* (New York,
1961), pp. 94–95.

Perhaps this has always been so except in the few great eras of the drama.

Thus far, I have examined the drama of ideas from a positive standpoint, as a conflict of ideas, or rather, ideals. But there is also a negative way of viewing the whole question, one which Eric Bentley sums up in the words "the lack of a common faith." This phrase occurs in his discussion of Lessing, who, he says,

> must surely be the first major writer to see quite clearly that . . . there could be a drama in which the basic conflict was one of ideas, and that such a drama might be peculiarly appropriate to a world without a common faith, philosophy, or idea.[15]

Hebbel's theories of drama, as expounded by Mr. Bentley, reinforce Lessing's:

> Great drama, [Hebbel] maintained, occurred at the transition from one epoch to the next and expressed the clash of *Weltanschauungen*—"world views." So far Western history had known two such crises. The first was when the antique world shifted from simplicity to reflection, from belief in gods to belief in fate. The second was when the medieval order was shaken by the individualism of the Protestants.[16]

Hebbel identified a third crisis in the nineteenth century, but I do not think we ought to follow him there, for the second crisis

[15] *The Playwright As Thinker*, p. 51.
[16] *Ibid.*, pp. 28–29.

has in fact never ended. Since the sixteenth century, Western civilization has been in perpetual crisis through lack of a common faith; it follows that the conditions for drama of ideas, perhaps even for great drama, have been constantly present for the past four centuries. True, there have been moments of stability when drama of ideas went into eclipse, but these were merely local and temporary.

In periods when members of the middle class formed the great majority of theatergoers and supplied all the playwrights, it was possible to treat certain bourgeois assumptions as the eternal verities. The ethos of another class, culture, or nationality was only admitted to the stage on the condition that it should be either condemned or ridiculed. This stability never lasted, however, because the middle class itself became fragmented. Trite as it may sound, the newspaper, the railroad, the telegraph, and the steamboat made possible the drama of Ibsen. How many references we find in his plays to newspaper editorials and to foreign travel! Oswald Alving, like several other Ibsen characters, has been to Paris. In the late nineteenth century the tight, puritanical homogeneity of the Norwegian small town began to disintegrate. It was not only that middle-class people realized they no longer all shared the same ideals; they found that they did not all *behave* in the same way either.

Shaw, with his acute sociological awareness, made use of this fact in developing a peculiarly Shavian hybrid between the drama of ideas and the comedy of manners. In a whole series of his plays the questions "What should I believe?" and "How should I behave in company?" are deliberately confused, or, rather, shown to be one and the same question. *You Never Can Tell* is the first of a series that includes *Getting Married* and *Misalliance* and culminates in *Heartbreak House*. Since this last play is usually regarded as a Chekhovian tragicomedy, a brief analysis of it from the standpoint of comedy of manners seems necessary here. It is no more paradoxical to relate drama of ideas to comedy of manners than it is to relate Restoration comedy of manners to drama of ideas.

Heartbreak House, the ship-shaped dwelling where octogenarian Captain Shotover lives with his daughter Hesione, his son-in-law Hector Hushabye, and old Nurse Guinness, has its own sophisticated code—"our family habit of throwing stones in all directions and letting the air in." To this house come three unsophisticated middle-class characters: young Ellie Dunn, her inventor father, and her suitor, "Boss" Mangan. At first they feel completely at a loss in the happy-go-lucky, amoral household, but eventually Mazzini Dunn and his daughter come to terms with it. Mangan, a British Cabinet Minister and moderately crooked financier, does not. At one point he becomes so exasperated that he starts tearing off his clothes:

> Let's all strip stark naked. . . . We've stripped ourselves morally naked: well, let us strip ourselves physically naked as well and see how we like it. I tell you I can't bear this. I was brought up to be respectable. I don't mind the women dyeing their hair and the men drinking: it's human nature. But it's not human nature to tell everybody about it. . . . How are we to have any self-respect if we don't keep it up that we're better than we really are?

By contrast, Mazzini Dunn, inventor and dreamer, is quite at home. "Where else," he asks, "could I feel perfectly at ease in my pyjamas? . . . . You are very charming people, most advanced, unprejudiced, frank, humane, unconventional, democratic, free-thinking, and everything that is delightful to thoughtful people."

Two conventional upper-class people also enter this enchanted society from outside: Lady Utterword, who is Hesione's sister, and her brother-in-law and lover, Randall Utterword. Lady Utterword's one desire as a child had been to escape from her disorderly home to a completely conventional environment, but she is not shocked by Heartbreak House, as Mangan is, for she was born in it. On the other hand, she is not fascinated by it as Mazzini and Ellie are: "I know by experience," she says, "that men and women are tender plants and must be cultivated under glass." She tells Dunn that, if he were to stay at her house:

> I should make you very comfortable; and you would not have the trouble and anxiety of wondering whether you should wear your purple and gold or your green and crimson dressing-gown at dinner. You complicate life instead of simplifying it by doing these ridiculous things.

She it is who says that "there are only two classes in good society in England, the equestrian classes and the neurotic classes." In his preface Shaw calls them "Horseback Hall" and "Heartbreak House." There, he does not approve of either, but he tends to favor the horsey people as being doers of deeds, even though brainless ones; the neurotic classes may be thinkers, but they *do* nothing.

In the play, the spectator or reader must make his own choice between the two ways of life. I suspect that, on the whole, the

Heartbreak House people attract Shaw's unconscious sympathies. In the German air raid at the end of the play, the only ones to be killed are Mangan and a burglar. Still, the Heartbreak House characters, true to type, view the raid solely as an aesthetic experience. Hesione speaks for them all when she says: "But what a glorious experience! I hope they'll come again tomorrow night."

Actually, if one thinks the play over, one finds not merely two ways of life but three or four: conventional upper-class, bohemian upper-class, conventional middle-class, and (if we count the burglar) unconventional lower-class. Shavian comedy of manners presents a plural society, leaving us to choose which ethos we prefer or, possibly, to construct our own synthesis from the best elements of the codes set before us. Such a play as *Heartbreak House* could make no sense in a unified culture, but it makes very good sense in one like ours, which some people rather pretentiously call "pluralistic." Plural or pluralistic or fragmented, such is the culture in which we are immersed; the drama of ideas is, I believe, its most appropriate expression.

Any contemporary playwright who rejects the drama of ideas is also rejecting our society. Perforce, he is trying to set up a new orthodoxy, a new myth, or else to revive an old one. A Claudel writes within the framework of Catholicism, a Brecht within that of Communism. A Yeats writes within the framework of an imagined Unity of Being older than Christianity. The history of the Abbey Theatre during Yeats's lifetime presents a unique example of a theater censored from within while battling furiously against censorship from without. From the days of his break with Edward Martyn and George Moore down to his rejection of O'Casey's *The Silver Tassie,* Yeats fought valiantly against Ibsenism and the drama of ideas generally. He professed to despise Ibsen and his followers for the poverty of their language, but in truth it was their pluralism, their negation of the Unity of Being, that he detested.

Existentialism, whose fundamental tenet is that nothing is given, ought to show a firm commitment, both in theory and practice, to drama of ideas. In practice, the basic conflict has been existentialism versus everything else. In theory, since no possible course of action can be ruled out a priori in a particular situation, pluralism ought to have free rein. However, a logical difficulty arises: if one really has no preconceptions, what conflict of ideas is possible over the merits of choosing one course of action rather than another?

To conclude, then, so long as Western man—or contemporary Eastern man, for that matter—continues to lack a common faith, I see no possibility that the drama of ideas can become wholly obsolete. No, I am wrong. There is one contradictory possibility. Suppose that man, confronted with an infinite variety of choices, all equally attractive or repellent, finally lost the will to act at all. Then there could be no drama, of ideas or otherwise. However, during the brief interval of consciousness which remained to him, man could still tell himself stories mentally. Those stories, produced without the aid of articulate writing or speech, might strangely resemble some of the novels and plays of Samuel Beckett.

JOHN GASSNER

❦

# Shaw on Ibsen and the Drama of Ideas

The rise of distinctively modern drama is usually associated with the development of "drama of ideas" during the last third of the nineteenth century. This is virtually an article of faith among theater historians, and it has been left intact by a succession of revolutions in dramatic theory and criticism. Ibsen, it is maintained, created the genre of drama of ideas; Shaw promulgated and developed it. Ibsen was the creator, and Shaw was his prophet. In the English-speaking world there could be no doubt about the accuracy of either statement by the end of the nineteenth or the beginning of the twentieth century. Shaw's role was evident wherever Shaw's dramatic criticism penetrated and his early plays were seen or read. As for Ibsen's role, it could not be questioned by anyone startled by the content of Ibsen's plays, since drama of ideas meant, of course, drama of ideas that called attention to themselves.

These are, obviously, transparent simplifications. Shaw's advocacy of Ibsen was by no means the sole or even the first factor in the gradual acceptance of Ibsen as a major playwright in England. His interpretation of Ibsen's plays could be questioned, not to say improved upon, and it was not difficult to conclude that Shaw as critic and champion had created an ideal in his own image. It used to be said that his *Quintessence of Ibsenism* was actually a "Quintessence of Shavianism." If Shaw was useful to Ibsen as an advocate, Ibsen was useful to Shaw as a post-fabricated forerunner. It was certainly unnecessary to accept Shaw in order to accept Ibsen, and a close student of the latter, such as William Archer, could not fail to realize that Ibsen and Shaw were two different breeds of men who differed radically in their dramatic artistry. But this much is certain: the concept of drama of ideas was to a considerable degree Shaw's contribution to dramatic theory; it was, in part, a Shavian discovery and, in part, a Shavian invention useful in the struggle for liberal principles and modern social drama.

To observe this phenomenon adequately we must do several things that cannot possibly be accomplished in a single paper. We must compare Ibsen's plays with Shaw's exegesis, which is no mean assignment, chiefly because of what Shaw left out of consideration more or less deliberately. We cannot confidently match Ibsen's intentions with the intentions blithely attributed to him by Shaw, who spoke as one unacquainted with the obscure night of the soul of one of the theater's most ambivalence-ridden authors. Shaw is not necessarily wrong or obtuse, but much that seems crystal-clear in a short Shavian analysis or synopsis of one of Ibsen's plays proves to be decidedly complicated and somewhat murky in the play itself.

In the history of Shaw's concern with Ibsen as "the onlie begetter" of modern drama of ideas it is, moreover, helpful to discriminate three main stages. The first appears when Shaw speaks on Ibsen to the Fabian Soceity in 1890 and publishes his lectures in 1891 under the title of *The Quintessence of Ibsenism;* the second, when Shaw, covering the London theater between 1895 and 1898 for Frank Harris's periodical *The Saturday Review,* serves Ibsen in commenting on Ibsen productions, as well as on the plays of pre-Ibsenist playwrights such as Sardou and pseudo-Ibsenite dramatists such as Pinero; the third, when after long practice as a playwright himself and considerable observation of the theater since his retirement from *The Saturday Review* in favor of Max Beerbohm, Shaw brings out a new edition of *The Quintessence of Ibsenism* in 1913. He brings this publication up to date by adding a section on Ibsen's last four plays (*The Master Builder, Little Eyolf, John Gabriel Borkman,* and *When We Dead Awaken*), published after Shaw's Fabian lecture, and develops his conception of drama of ideas by providing two new concluding chapters. In the first stage, Shaw writes as a Fabian reformer; in the second, as a journalist reviewer; in the third, as a critic and historian of the drama. In the first two stages he was effective (with others) in securing a victory for Ibsen in England. In the third stage he reflected on the victory, defined its nature, and described it as the decisive event in the making of modern drama.

Half a century has elapsed since then—a rather large interval of time in the life of literary theory and practice. It is hardly too soon, therefore, to reexamine Shaw's conception of drama of ideas and to test its application to the work of Ibsen and his successors. By piecing together Shaw's viewpoint from the aforementioned three stages of his engagement with Ibsen, we may hope to achieve a perspective that Shaw himself would not find objectionable, although nothing is more certain than Shaw's great disinterest in dramatic theory per se unless it is his readiness to resort to theory as an instrument of his Socialist and argumentative inclinations.

As Shaw tells us himself, *The Quintessence of Ibsen* was

originally a *pièce d'occasion*. The Fabian Society decided to
occupy its membership during the summer of 1890 with a series
of lectures under the general title of "Socialism in Contemporary
Literature," and Shaw volunteered to speak on Ibsen. His lecture
was "duly read at the St. James's Restaurant on the 18th of July,"
and as duly laid aside by its author, who was probably correct in
concluding that the series had added "nothing to the general
stock of information on Socialism in Contemporary Literature."
He decided to publish the lecture in 1891 only after concluding,
as a result of disputes over Ibsen's plays, that an exposition of
Ibsenism was greatly needed. *Rosmersholm,* produced at the
Vaudeville Theatre by Florence Farr, *Ghosts,* presented as the
inaugural production of the Independent Theatre, and *Hedda
Gabler,* he recalled, had "started a frantic newspaper controversy,
in which I could see no sign of any of the disputants having ever
been forced by circumstances, as I had, to make up his mind
definitely as to what Ibsen's plays meant." [1] Shaw proceeded to
give his views to the public after candidly warning his readers
in the Preface that he had not written "a critical essay on the
poetic beauties of Ibsen, but simply an exposition of Ibsenism."
He also admitted that his conclusions were drawn from the plays
rather than from explicit comments by Ibsen himself—that, as

---

[1] G. B. Shaw, *The Quintessence of Ibsenism* (New York, 1914), Preface,
p. vi. Also, Shaw's *Major Critical Essays* (London, 1932), pp. 11–12. As a
partisan for the luminous known and the readily manifest, Shaw could not,
of course, evince much patience for anyone ill at ease in the presence
of the dark unknown in Ibsen's work that made Henry James, for example,
complain of Ibsen's "bewildering incongruities" in *Hedda Gabler* and refer
to his "strangely inscrutable art" in *The Master Builder*.

Shaw put it, "the existence of a discoverable and perfectly definite thesis in a poet's work by no means depends on the completeness of his own intellectual consciousness of it." [2]

The essence of Ibsenism, according to Shaw, is that Ibsen offends his opponents and pleases his supporters because his plays invalidate old beliefs and propose new ones. His struggles and questionings propound a transvaluation of values in the interests of progress. For Shaw, echoing Marx, Butler, Nietzsche, and other leaders of nineteenth century iconoclasm, "progress must involve the repudiation of an established duty at every step," and there is nothing new in "the defiance of duty by the reformer: Every step of progress means a duty repudiated and a scripture torn up." [3] This view is maintained against a representative of conservative dramatic criticism, Clement Scott, who led the opposition to Ibsen in London and demanded the suppression of *Ghosts* in the British theater on the grounds that he, as spectator, has been exhorted by Ibsen "to laugh at honor, to disbelieve in love, to mock at virtue, to distrust friendship, and to deride fidelity." [4] It is plain then, that Shaw acclaimed Ibsen as a revolutionist and that drama of ideas could mean but one thing to Shaw, namely, subversive drama; for surely Clement Scott and his numerous followers also had "ideas," but conservative ones. Had these latter been expressed or demonstrated in a play, we may well ask, would they have qualified the play as a drama of

[2] *Ibid.* This was a sound precaution, since Ibsen himself was inclined to disclaim political partisanship or any strong opinion.

[3] *Major Critical Essays*, p. 17.

[4] *Ibid.*, p. 15.

ideas? Apparently not! For the operative word "ideas" we would
have to substitute the word "challenges" to approximate Shaw's
meaning.

This was tantamount to saying that a conservative position
could not produce drama of ideas or had no ideas worthy of a
modern intellect, a point of view to which Gilbert Chesterton,
T. E. Hulme, T. S. Eliot, and later neoconservatives could justifi-
ably take exception. It could be argued that Shaw had got himself
caught in a trap of his own devising in substituting an illiberalism
of the Left for the illiberalism of the Right. This argument would
not have disturbed Shaw, however, because he thought of criticism as a partisan tactic rather than as an end in itself. He was
by training and inclination a debater rather than an arbitrator;
and he was far more interested in disparaging Victorian moralism
than in maintaining the dubious virtue of consistency.

It is also conceivable that conservatives reacting at a later time
to a *status quo* of liberalism might take the offensive in the manner of T. S. Eliot's attacks on democratic disunity or, as he calls it
in *The Idea of a Christian Society,* "a liberalized or negative condition of society." [5] But this eventuality would not have disconcerted the later Shaw, who became perfectly aware of flaws in
democracy and hankered for government by superior individuals.
His thinking was, as a rule, relativistic rather than absolutist, and
he would have had no difficulty in admitting to the category of
drama of ideas, at some later time than the 1890s, a play that
*reversed* belief in the inevitability of progress and the worth of
democratic government. In his old age he wrote such plays himself (*The Apple Cart, Too True to Be Good, On the Rocks,* and

[5] *The Idea of a Christian Society* (New York, 1940), p. 23.

*The Millionairess*) without in the least depriving them of provocative ideas—which did not, however, make him revise his
premise of the 1890s that the only sound ideas were modern ones.
(It is this assumption that led him to assert superiority to Shakespeare in the realm of thought and to consider Ibsen "more
useful" for his times than Shakespeare, and more "useful," too,
than many a contemporary naturalist determined to record sordid
details, as, for example, Zola, about whom Ibsen is said to have
once declared "[He] descends into the cesspool to take a bath,
I to cleanse it." [6]

First, then, Shaw announced the principle of relativism in the
matter of morality and applied it to his defense of Ibsen against
the conservative opposition. Ibsen was praised, for having reduced
Victorian morality to a tragic absurdity in *Ghosts*. The heroine
in that play, Mrs. Alving, came to realize that she had been
grievously wrong in adhering to the puritanical code of her times
instead of leaving her profligate husband. The rewards of conventional virtue in her case had been years of humiliation in the
past and was a diseased son on the brink of feeblemindedness in
the present. If the worthy Victorian drama critic Clement Scott
had allowed himself to be upset by a production of *Ghosts* in
London to the point of wanting the authorities to withdraw the
offending theater's license, it was because the Victorian establish-
ment had yet to surrender the notion that morals are unchanging
and absolute in application. Ibsen's Mrs. Alving would have been
more moral if she had been less submissive to moralistic abso-
lutism in Norwegian society. Repudiation of "duty" by woman,
Ibsen's implicit theme in *A Doll's House* and *Ghosts,* was justified

[6] A. E. Zucker, *Ibsen the Master Builder* (New York, 1929), p. 181.

by Shaw as an instance of the general validity of rejecting out-worn mores and morals. The repudiation of established opinion and specious morality, we may note parenthetically, is recurrent in the work of latter-day practitioners of drama of ideas, such as Brecht and Sartre. Brecht's work often culminates in revolu-tionary irony; Sartre's in existentialist tragedy.

Shaw started his apology for Ibsen rather laboriously in a chapter entitled "The Two Pioneers," by distinguishing two different types of pioneer: the reformer who declares something to be right that had hitherto been regarded as infamous, and the revolutionist who declares something to be wrong that had hitherto been considered eminently right. He calls the former an "indulgence preacher" and the latter an "abstinence preacher," although a particular individual (the poet Shelley, for example) can be both an "indulgence preacher" and an "abstinence preacher" in differing respects. Still, nothing particularly original came from this distinction in *The Quintessence of Ibsenism*. Shaw was considerably more successful in the second chapter entitled "Ideals and Idealists," in which he divided men into three categories. There are the "Philistines," who are satisfied with things as they are and display neither intellectual curiosity nor artistic sensibility. They neither create nor challenge principles or ideals. Naturally, they constitute the great majority; in a thousand people, says Shaw, you are likely to find 700 Philistines. There are also the "Idealists" in considerable number (299 out of a thousand!) who mask realities with fancies and, says Shaw, "graft pleasure on necessity" with desperately defended illusions, making belief in them "a point of public decency." These are, in Shaw's terms, the idealists who are up in arms against Ibsen, who made

his outspoken character Dr. Relling in *The Wild Duck* declare
that "ideals" are pretenses and that a good old-fashioned Norwegian word for them is "lies"! And, finally, there is the third
category, to which a man like Ibsen and no doubt Shaw himself
belong, namely, the one man in a thousand whom Shaw calls a
"realist," who dares to pull the masks off things that idealists have
placed on them. For Ibsen and Shaw, then, the evil they fight is
"idealism," and the enemy they encounter is not the Philistine but
the idealist.

A pervasive anti-Victorian revolt, with or without Fabian Socialist overtones for which Ibsen's middle-class drama provided
hardly an occasion, would alone have provided a sufficient spring-
board for Shaw's advocacy of drama of ideas. So would have
Shaw's general craving for an intellectually stimulating theater,
into which he was ready to pour the varied substance of his reading and enthusiasms. It is no accident that his first play,
*Widower's Houses,* on which he had been working since 1885,
should have been completed and staged in London within a year
of the publication of *The Quintessence of Ibsenism.* But Shaw
gave the argument in that tract a special Shavian twist that we
can only ascribe to his gyroscopic intellect. He arrived at a
piquant formulation of Ibsenism by means of the semantic device
of calling conservative thinking like Clement Scott's idealism,
and iconoclastic thinking like his own and Ibsen's realism. Some
forensic advantages were patently inherent in a formulation that
revised the usual nomenclature for conservatism and radicalism;
here was indeed an early instance of Shaw's trick of turning
things topsy-turvy that so upset his critics and delighted his admirers and that was surely as much a habit of mind as a calcula-

tion on his part. In any case, the novelty of Shaw's revisionist definition was bound to be arresting and its patent irony entertaining.

Shaw's introductory comments and the summaries of the plays that follow the chapter on "Ideals and Idealists" present Ibsen as an imaginative writer, albeit a rather thin playwright, rather than as a humdrum reformer. Many a scrupulously written later study, as well as many a stage production after 1890, was to do less than that. Ibsen would have had to wink a little when Shaw attributed a comprehensive philosophy to him not many years before he himself declared in a public address that he had been "more of a poet and less of a philosopher than is commonly supposed." But he could well have been pleased with the dramatic *élan* and acute intelligence attributed to him by Shavian exegesis.

It has been all too possible to treat Ibsen as a prosaic middle-class writer. Shaw's timely intervention in behalf of Ibsen's reputation saved it from possible imputation of dullness. If there had been a grain of Shavian wit indeed among the outraged conservatives who flouted Ibsen as the Devil incarnate, they could have exchanged their hysterical denunciations for Shavian complaints that the Devil was too unexciting and dull for them. They could have disposed of modern drama of ideas altogether by charging intellectual playwrights with static playwriting, argumentativeness rather than dramatic action, desiccation of feeling, and the substitution of mouthpieces for characters. This is the kind of criticism to which Shaw and many later dramatists of ideas such as Granville Barker, Pirandello, Brecht, and Sartre were, indeed, to be exposed at one time or another. We may observe parenthetically that the best butt of truly Shavian criticism, curiously enough, turned out to be Shaw himself when he became the subject of a brilliant little book by G. K. Chesterton in 1909. Chesterton accused Shaw of an insufficient sense of paradox and of not quite understanding life because Shaw "will not accept its contradictions." Chesterton took pains to explain early in his book that by paradox he meant "truth inherent in a paradox" rather than simply "something that makes one jump," and he concluded that Shaw's "madness is all consistency, not inconsistency." [7]

An illustration of Shavian exegesis is Shaw's previously mentioned treatment of *Ghosts,* which was watered down into a second-rate tract on the dangers of heredity in more than one instance of both favorable and hostile criticism. Ibsen's admirers and followers were, in fact, especially inclined to interpret *Ghosts* as a naturalistic sermon and to imitate it as such. Hauptmann reflected this view when he started his dramatic career in 1889 with *Before Sunrise,* a crude naturalistic *piéce à thèse,* in which the hero refuses to marry the heroine because there is alcoholism in her family; and Echegaray won a specious reputation for modernism in the Spanish theater with another variation on the heredity theme, *The Son of Don Juan,* in which Don Juan, now middle-aged and respectable, receives condign punishment for the profligacy of his youth when his about-to-be-married son turns out to be diseased.

It is refreshing to come across Shaw's comments on *Ghosts* after considerable unevenness in the early chapters of his discourse on Ibsen's play. This begins with a little chapter on Ibsen's *Brand*

[7] G. K. Chesterton, ed., *George Bernard Shaw* (London, 1948), pp. 173, 175, 177.

that presents an almost complete distortion of the play, although there is some evidence that he appreciated Brand as an heroic figure.[8] His next chapter on *Peer Gynt* appreciates the irony in that work and its reductive treatment of Peer the would-be self-realizer as a prototype, Shaw says, of "the pushing, competitive, success-craving man who is the hero of the modern world." In Peer the characterless loafer and shabby opportunist, the idealizing tendency turns out to be nothing but "the romantic fancies of the born liar," and Peer's conception of himself as "a self-realized man" is exposed in the play as sheer self-delusion. In Shaw's acute little chapter, moreover, we get inklings of the possibility of having drama of ideas in poetic and fantastic form, that is, of not having to identify or associate this genre with problem plays and prosaic playwriting. Shaw does not make this point himself, but, as we may observe in his appreciation of the intellectual vitality of *Peer Gynt* as well as in his own later practice as a playwright whenever he resorted to fancy or extravagance, drama of ideas is anything but a restrictive genre. Those who would limit it to prosaic argument have not read Shaw well either as a critic or a playwright.

Shaw's next chapter, on Ibsen's *Emperor and Galilean,* is unsatisfactory. There is no flagrant distortion here, but considerable confusion, partly produced by Ibsen's historical double-drama itself and partly by Shaw's zealous recourse to Victorian free-thinking and protest against the quasi-Darwinist doctrine of

[8] *Major Critical Essays,* p. 48 ("Brand, made terrible by the consequences of his idealism to others, is heroic"), and p. 51 ("It is against this conception of God as a sentimental dupe that Brand rages"). See also the beginning of the second paragraph on p. 42.

Natural Selection in sociology with its fatalistic *laissez-faire* doctrine of the "survival of the fittest" in society. Shaw's remarks are
relevant to elucidation of *Emperor and Galilean* only when he
refers directly to the character of Julian the Apostate, whom he
aptly, if not altogether justly, defines as an early Peer Gynt.[9]
The Emperor Julian, Shaw says, is with respect to the "antithesis
between idealism and realism . . . a reincarnation of Peer Gynt."

Shaw insists on forcing *Brand, Peer Gynt* and *Emperor and
Galilean* into the mold of his thesis by referring to them as "three
immense dramas, all dealing with the effect of idealism on individual egotists of exceptional imaginative excitability." And
Shaw justifies the liberties he was taking in interpreting these
plays by declaring that at the time of their creation Ibsen was still
a subjective writer; his "intellectual consciousness of his theme
was yet incomplete"; he was still "simply portraying sides of
himself." Not so in the prose plays that followed *Emperor and
Galilean,* according to Shaw, because Ibsen, "having at last completed his intellectual analysis of idealism . . . could now construct methodical illustrations of its social working." In the plays of
the postromantic middle period, says Shaw, "Ibsen could see
plainly the effect of idealism [the effect, that is, of masking
reality] as a social force on . . . everyday people in everyday life,"
and not merely on "saints, romantic adventurers, and emperors." [10]

This procedure started with Ibsen's satiric comedy *The League
of Youth* in 1869 and more distinctly with the "first of the series of
realistic prose plays," *Pillars of Society* in 1877, and, two years later,
*A Doll's House*. And so impressive were the plays that followed

[9] *Ibid.*, pp. 55, 59.
[10] *Ibid.*, p. 60.

in the Ibsen canon that neglect or scorn of the work of Dumas *fils,* Émile Augier, and other early problem play writers could seduce one into believing that drama of ideas began its association with the realistic theater in Ibsen's work. This is not the case, of course. Friedrich Hebbel, in reflecting Hegelian philosophy, for which he entertained a high regard, presented a conflict between old ideas and new as early as 1844, in his middle-class tragedy *Maria Magdalena;* and Hebbel made an important early observation concerning drama of ideas in his *Journals* when he wrote that "drama should not present new stories but new relationships," and that "ideas are to the drama what counterpoint is to music. In themselves nothing but the *sine qua non* for everything." [11]

There seems to be no evidence that Shaw was familiar with Hebbel's *Maria Magdalena.* The work of Dumas *fils,* however, was well known to Shaw. The younger Dumas began to write social drama almost as a journalist by about the middle of the nineteenth century and dealt with contemporary problems in *The Demi-Monde, The Question of Money,* and other once popular plays. A more skillful playwright, Émile Augier, followed him with topical plays such as *La Jeunesse,* an attack on materialism in society, and *Les Effrontés,* an exposé of yellow journalism. Dumas *fils,* in fact, came out strongly for drama of ideas, which he equated with moral and *useful* drama, in an open letter to the Parisian critic Sarcey.[12] If he could treat causes rather than merely effects, and if he could find the means to force people

[11] *Playwrights on Playwriting,* ed. Toby Cole (New York, 1959), pp. 287–88.

[12] Published in *Entr'actes* (Paris, 1877), and quoted in Barrett H. Clark's

to discuss a problem and lawmakers to revise a particular law, he would be doing his part as a man as well as a poet. There was, of course, no poetry in such plays, only the surface realism of commonplace verisimilitude; and it is chiefly this kind of social drama that prevails even today, varying only in degree of characterization and intensity of conflict. But Shaw could not be impressed with Dumas *fils,* because he devised intricate plots instead of providing provocative discussions and was humdrum rather than revolutionary in his thinking. The latter still employed the so-called well-made play technique, which emphasized a contrived and involved plot, popularized since the 1840s by Eugène Scribe. Moreover, the reforms advocated by the younger Dumas barely scratched the surface of society. It seemed, on the contrary, that the consuming interest of Dumas, Augier, and other pre-Ibsenite playwrights, as well as post-Ibsenite ones led in England by Pinero, was to defend middle-class interests and morals. If "ideas" functioned in their plays at all, they were conventional ones; like the late Calvin Coolidge's New England clergyman, they were simply against sin. (And since the sin was usually adultery, the scholar-critic Gilbert Norwood was once justified in claiming that they had reduced the Decalogue to a monologue.)[13] For Shaw, socially effective drama of ideas started not simply when Ibsen gave up writing verse drama and turned to everyday life and conversation, but when the drama became

---

*European Theories of the Drama, with a Supplement in the American Drama* (New York, 1947), p. 382.

[13] Gilbert Norwood in *Euripides and Shaw* (Boston, 1911), p. 65. Norwood wrote: "Your pseudo-advanced writer invariably reveals his calibre by this assumption that 'the problem-play' must treat of marital infidelity: there is only one sin—the Decalogue has become a monologue."

acutely critical rather than routinely reformatory and replaced interest in plot with interest in inquiry, conflict of values or ideas, and discursive action—that is, action of the intelligence.

This change was first apparent in *A Doll's House,* the full significance of which Shaw did not formulate as clear theory until some twenty-two years after his Fabian lecture, when he came to amplify *The Quintessence of Ibsenism* for a revised edition published in 1913. In the 1891 edition Shaw made some excellent small points. He pointed out, for example, that, whereas the fraudulent hero of *Pillars of Society* was a pillar only in the ironical sense of the word, the Philistine husband in *A Doll's House,* "the pillar of society who owns the doll," was by conventional standards "a model husband, father, and citizen." [14] But it is first in a chapter added to the 1913 edition, called "The Technical Novelty in Ibsen's Plays" [15] that Shaw made the important observation that a "new technical factor," the element of discussion, entered the theater with *A Doll's House* and won a dominant position in the drama. Shaw's summation is too important not to be given *in toto:*

This technical factor in the play is the discussion. Formerly you had in what was called a well-made play an exposition in the first act, a situation in the second, and unravelling in the third. Now you have exposition, situation, and discussion; and the discussion is the test of the playwright. The critics protest in vain. They declare that discussions are not dramatic, and that art should not be didactic. Neither the playwrights nor the

[14] *Major Critical Essays,* p. 64.
[15] *Ibid.,* p. 135.

public take the smallest notice of them. The discussion conquered Europe in Ibsen's *A Doll's House;* and now the serious
playwright recognizes in the discussion not only the main test
of his highest powers, but also the real centre of his play's interest. . . . This was inevitable if the drama was ever again
to be raised above the childish demand for fables without
morals.[16]

Shaw went on to explain that the ordinary plot-play, the drama-
tized fable that does not rise above "the commonplaces of the
Newgate Calendar," would simply have to go, because intrigues
and story contrivances were soon exhausted: "In twenty visits
[to the theatre] one can see every possible change rung on all the
available plots and incidents out of which plays of this kind can
be manufactured." [17] And at this point we once more encounter
evidence to the effect that it is not realistic technique or style that
Shaw considers paramount in modern drama, whether by Ibsen
or himself, but realism of viewpoint.

Early critics of Shaw could indeed go further and affect to
regard the bulk of his dramatic writing as fantastic, a view
pleasantly sustained by Gilbert Chesterton while complimenting
Shaw for excelling in "the difficult art of being at once modern
and intelligent." This, indeed, was the burden of A. B. Walkley's
clever review of a revival of *Candida* at the Court Theatre in the
spring of 1904. The first paragraph of Walkley's review reads:

Fantasy has its place in the theatre, as well as realism, and that
is one reason why the theatre has room for Mr. Bernard Shaw.

[16] *Ibid.*
[17] *Ibid.*, p. 136.

His method of travestying life is to eliminate from it everything but pure intelligence. Just as Mr. H. G. Wells amuses us by supposing a world where the laws of gravity are suspended, or where there is no such thing as time or where space is of $X$ dimensions, so Mr. Shaw amuses us by representing a world where conduct is regulated by thought, and men love women, as the civil servant in Pickwick ate crumpets, on principle.[18]

Walkley, reflecting that "our little exploits of coherent thought are mere bobbing corks on the great stream of life," concluded not unexpectedly that "the chief delight" of Shaw's plays was their "brilliant dialectics," and that on the whole *Candida* on the stage is "capital sport." He observed, it is true, that "Mr. Shaw takes care to give his fantasy a certain admixture of reality," as in the case of the recognizable parson Morell and of Candida herself as "the managing, mothering, thoroughly competent woman, who carries about innumerable bags and parcels, with an aggressive air of brisk usefulness, and cannot talk to a man without patting him on the back, or retying his cravat, or picking bits of cotton off his coat." And Walkley knew well enough that for Shaw's plays to be regarded as "capital sport" was not in the least satisfactory to Shaw. "Mr. Shaw," he wrote, "maintains that he is quite serious, an out-and-out realist; in short, that in saluting him as a merry sportsman one is like the young lady who when [the Reverend] Sydney Smith said grace, shook him by the hand with a 'Thank you so much, Mr. Smith; you are always so amusing.' " [19]

[18] A. B. Walkley, *Drama and Life* (New York, 1908), p. 214.
[19] *Ibid.,* pp. 214–18.

Walkley scores well here, and Shaw's view of himself as a realist extends to Ibsen in all editions of *The Quintessence of Ibsenism*. This may be observed in his summary of the dramatic action of *The Lady from the Sea*,[20] in which Ibsen's play is shorn of all its fancifulness and mystery, and of all its poetry too, in the interest of elementary clarity and humdrum credibility.

Shaw must have been himself aware that in explicating this play he was explaining away both its defect of mistiness and its merit of poetry or apt symbolism, just as he had underrated the poetry and imaginativeness of *Peer Gynt* in an earlier chapter. Referring to Ellida, the respectably married heroine of *The Lady from the Sea,* who is mysteriously drawn to the sea and is claimed by a sailor with "fish eyes," Shaw wrote that "she seems more fantastic to English readers than to Norwegian ones" and that "the same thing is true of many other characters drawn by Ibsen, notably Peer Gynt, who, if born in England, would certainly not have been a poet and metaphysician as well as a blackguard and a speculator." Shaw took exception to the tendency of British audiences to consider *Rosmersholm* and *The Lady from the Sea* as "more fantastic and less literal than *A Doll's House* and the plays in which the leading figures are men and women of action."[21] And in making this evaluation he did not differ greatly with Ibsen himself, even though the latter preferred to be considered a poet and not a realistic reformer. Ibsen does not appear to have drawn a sharp distinction between the plays of his middle period and the more or less symbolist works of his last period: *The Master Builder, Little Eyolf, John Gabriel Borkman,* and

[20] *Major Critical Essays,* p. 82.
[21] *Ibid.,* pp. 84–85.

*When We Dead Awaken,* published between 1892 and 1900. The latter-day Ibsen did not enroll himself under the banner of the symbolists, even though they laid claim to him.

Maeterlinck's manifesto of the year 1896, "The Tragical in Daily Life," concludes with complimentary paragraphs on *The Wild Duck.* Maeterlinck referred to Ibsen as "the old master" who "freed certain powers of the soul that have never yet been free" and whose protagonists Hilda and Solness in *The Master Builder* were "the first characters in drama who feel . . . that they are living in the atmosphere of the soul." [22] There is, however, no evidence that Ibsen thought of himself as a symbolist when he invented the "white horses" of *Rosmersholm,* the wounded bird of *The Wild Duck,* or even the weird Rat Wife of *Little Eyolf.* Ibsen simply worked with whatever means were available to his imagination in elaborating and reinforcing a dramatic idea in a particular play. And he composed all his last plays, except *When We Dead Awaken,* with a realist's firm grasp on characterization.

But it is idle, if not in fact misleading, to raise the issue of realism here at all in the sense of verisimilitude and literalism, and this may be said no less of Shaw's own plays. For Shaw simply did not insist, as a Galsworthy would have, that the realism that really mattered, namely, realism of idea or viewpoint, was necessarily dependent on verisimilitude. Like Brecht, who opposed Stanislavskian acting and realistic "dramaturgy" several decades later, Shaw showed no inclination to accept the illusion-

[22] Maurice Maeterlinck, "The Tragical in Daily Life" (*Le Tragique quotidien,* 1896), in *The Treasure of the Humble* (New York, 1907).

fostering machinery of theater already well exploited in unintellectual Victorian melodramas and pantomimes as a substitute for strenuous analysis and disputation. The need for maintaining illusion was not to be allowed to serve as a deterrent to "discussion drama," if Shaw could help it. So, returning in 1913 to the campaign he had waged as a partisan drama critic of the 1890s against contrived surface-realism more than fifteen years before and sounding rather like Dr. Samuel Johnson defending Shakespeare against the proponents of neoclassicism, Shaw proclaimed in the chapter on "The Technical Novelty in Ibsen's Plays" that "the illusion of reality is soon lost; in fact it may be doubted whether any adult ever entertains it; it is only to very young children that the fairy queen is anything but an actress." Only drama of ideas or discussion drama indeed can effectively displace the old-fashioned plays with involved plots full of what he called "the tomfooleries of action." Until fairly late in *A Doll's House,* Shaw declares in the new chapter, Ibsen's feminist play "might be turned into a very ordinary French drama by the excision of a few lines and the substitution of a sentimental happy ending for the famous last scene; indeed the very first thing the theatrical wiseacres did with it was to effect exactly this transformation."

A case in point, with which Shaw may have been unfamiliar, was the production of *A Doll's House* toured in the United States by the Polish actress Helena Modjeska in 1883 under the odd title of *Thora.* A reviewer for the Louisville *Courier-Journal,* who complained that the maimed play ended turgidly, provided a description of this ending, which resembled thousands of other play endings before and after Ibsen: Nora, here called Thora, "dons a street dress, and announces her intention of leaving her husband for ever. He expostulates, argues, and pleads in vain, but finally, through the medium of the children, some indefinite talk about 'religion,' there is a reunion and a falling curtain on a happy family tableau." [23]

"But," declares Shaw, "at just that point in the last act, the heroine very unexpectedly (by the wiseacres) stops her emotional acting, and says: 'We must sit down and discuss all this that has been happening between us.'" (Here the approving Shaw sounds as if he were anticipating Bertolt Brecht's theory of alienation, or *Verfremdung*. The emotional bond is abruptly broken while the plot-action is interrupted in order that the spectator, repossessing his judgment from pure emotional involvement and mere absorption in the story, may start thinking and arrive at some judgment.) With Nora's sitting down and reexamining her marriage, there begins a new phase in European drama in which it was modernized far more by Shaw himself, along with Granville Barker, Galsworthy, Cocteau, Giraudoux, Sartre, Brecht, and others than by the merely technical innovators of naturalist, symbolist, and expressionist persuasion. As Shaw put it in 1912: "And it was by this new technical feature: this addition of a new movement, as musicians would say, to the dramatic form, that *A Doll's House* conquered Europe and founded a new school of dramatic art." [24]

Shaw, however, noticed a further development. "Since that

[23] This review appears in *The American Theatre as Seen by its Critics*, ed. by Montrose J. Moses and John Mason Brown (New York, 1934).
[24] *Major Critical Essays*, p. 138.

time [since the writing of *A Doll's House*]," he continued, "the discussion has expanded far beyond the limits of an otherwise 'well-made' play." A disadvantage of placing the discussion at the end was that it would be necessary to see the play for a second time if one was to follow the earlier acts in the light of the final discussion. The theater, he observed, now (by 1913) has plays including some of his own, "which begin with discussion and end with action, and others in which the discussion inter-penetrates the action from the beginning to the end." [25]

In the new art beginning with *Ghosts,* the drama arises "through a conflict of unsettled ideals rather than through vulgar attachments, rapacities, generosities, resentments, ambitions, mis-understandings, oddities and so forth as to which no moral ques-tion is raised." Remembering Hegel perhaps as much as Ibsen, paralleling indeed Hegel's view that contradiction is the power that moves things and the Hegelian theory that tragedy is a conflict between two rights as exemplified in the *Antigone,* [26] Shaw elaborated upon his notion of a conflict of unsettled ideals: the conflict is "not between clear right and wrong; the villain is as conscientious as the hero, if not more so"—which is actually the case in Shaw's *Major Barbara,* in which Shaw makes out a better case for the munitions manufacturer Andrew Undershaft than for the Salvation Army. "Or," adds Shaw, "there are no villains and no heroes" in the new kind of discussion play, which

[25] *Ibid.* "Plays that begin with discussion and end with action" may not be easily cited, but this is approximately true of Shaw's *The Apple Cart, Man and Superman,* and *Major Barbara,* and Sartre's *The Flies.*

[26] See Hegel's *Philosophy of Art* and John Howard Lawson's *Theory and Technique of Playwriting* (New York, 1936).

he believes is exactly as it should be, as may be observed in the case of Hamlet, who would not have continued to hold our interest if he "never had any Ibsenist hesitations." [27]

According to Shaw, the one fault indeed to be found with Ibsen after *Ghosts* is that Ibsen still uses drastic *dénouements* such as may be found in the old-fashioned well-made plays. Shaw did not approve of Hedda's suicide at the conclusion of *Hedda Gabler* on the grounds that the really tragic fact about the Heddas of the world is not that they kill themselves but that they live on in all their aridity and uselessness. According to Shaw, "perhaps the most plausible reproach levelled at Ibsen by modern critics of his own school is just that survival of the old school in him which makes the death rate so high in his last acts," although he concedes that in Ibsen's latter-day work the play never exists for the sake of the catastrophe as it does in plays contrived solely for excitement. He cited the superior example of Chekhov's *The Cherry Orchard*—he was to emulate Chekhov a few years later in writing *Heartbreak House*—in which "the sentimental ideals of our amiable, cultured, Schumann-playing propertied class are reduced to dust and ashes by a hand not less deadly than Ibsen's because it is so much more caressing," a play in which "nothing more violent happens than that the family cannot afford to keep up its own house." Shaw maintains that it is "no true *dénouement* to cut the Gordian knot" and that "if people's souls are tied up by law or public opinion it is much more tragic to leave them wither in these bonds than to end their misery." [28] And Shaw indeed could have seen this viewpoint borne out before his death in

[27] *Major Critical Essays,* pp. 139, 142.
[28] *Ibid.,* pp. 142–43.

Brecht's *Mother Courage,* in which the title character resumes following camp after losing all her children in the Thirty Years' War, and in Sartre's *No Exit,* in which the characters are doomed to have to endure each other's company forever.

In the same 1913 chapter on Ibsen's drama of ideas as contrasted with drama of plot action, Shaw justifies himself as well as Ibsen in writing: "I myself have been reproached because the characters in my plays 'talk but do nothing,' meaning that they commit no felonies." And we may again observe that in championing Ibsen and post-Ibsen playwrights like himself, Shaw anticipated in 1913 the anti-Aristotelian protests and practices of later playwrights and directors such as Brecht, Piscator, Cocteau, Giraudoux, Jouvet, Anouilh, Adamov, and Wilder. "Hence a cry has arisen," Shaw declares, "that the post-Ibsen play is not a play, and that its technique, not being the technique described by Aristotle, is not a technique at all." [29]

Just as Brecht and Piscator both claimed that their "epic" theatrical form was not actually new but was rooted in older, indeed in classical, dramatic form, so Shaw reminds his critical sparring-partner Walkley that "the new technique is new only on the modern stage." It is as a means of demonstrating an idea or arguing about it, "the technique of playing upon the human conscience, and it has been practised by the playwright whenever the playwright has been capable of it." He then goes on to describe it, and it seems to me that actually the description fits no particular play by Ibsen after *Peer Gynt* and *Emperor and Galilean.* It does apply, however, to plays by Shaw, Strindberg (beginning with the expressionist trilogy *To Damascus*), Piran-

[29] *Ibid.,* pp. 143, 145–46.

dello, Auden, Eliot, Duerrenmatt, Frisch, Genêt, Beckett, Ionesco, and other modernists. He concludes:

"Rhetoric, irony, argument, paradox, epigram, parable, the rearrangement of haphazard facts into orderly and intelligent situations, these are both the oldest and the newest arts of the drama, and your plot construction and art of preparation are only the tricks of theatrical talent, the shifts of moral sterility, not the weapons of dramatic genius." [30]

And what better description can we have of Shaw's *Back to Methuselah* and *Heartbreak House* or Brecht's *The Caucasian Chalk Circle* and *The Good Woman of Setzuan,* which incidentally are both called "parable plays." How much less this summary applies to the dramatic form of Ibsen's postromantic plays is apparent. The variety of modernist types of dramatic structure, the deliberate theatricalization of reality in plays, the abrupt shifts from representational to presentational drama (that is, from illusionistic realism to direct address to the audience by some formal narrator, explicator, or choral character, as in Giraudoux's *Electra* and Anouilh's *Antigone*), the injection of illusion-breaking lyrics and choral recitations into the dramatic action (as in T. S. Eliot's *Murder in the Cathedral* and in Brecht's plays), and the pattern of moving into and out of illusion in the same play—one will look in vain in Ibsen's tightly built plays for these violations of realistic play structure, and for the naturalistic fourth-wall convention which completely separates the actor from his audience by hypostatizing a real wall between the two at the curtain line. From a technical standpoint we can only describe

[30] *Ibid.,* p. 146.

the postromantic Ibsen as moving stolidly from point to point to tell his story, create his characters, and establish his argument or analysis. We may watch his artistry with admiration as he conceals his tendentious art behind everyday details of life, credible characterization, and compressed prose dialogue, punctuated now and then with telling yet natural metaphors like Hedda's asking Lövborg to return to her from a stag party as a Dionysian figure wearing "vine-leaves" in his hair. And in passing, we may note how natural Ibsen's visual symbols are after *Peer Gynt,* so that they are indistinguishable from the dramatic action, as in the case of Nora's dancing the tarantella in *A Doll's House* in order to distract her husband, or from mere stage furnishings and stage properties, as in the case of the deceased General Gabler's portrait and his daughter's brace of pistols in *Hedda Gabler,* even if the pistols may be said to also "symbolize" Hedda's frigidity and destructiveness.

Nevertheless, Shaw was not wholly mistaken in attributing to Ibsen some of the elements he ascribed to the "new drama." They are not, it is true, formally, or stagily, striking, as when an actor in Giraudoux' *Electra* steps out of his role as Electra's gardener-fiancé when the engagement is called off and tells the audience in a Pirandellian manner that now that he is out of the play he can say what he thinks: "I'm not in the play any more. That's why I'm free to come and tell you what the play can't tell you." [31] But Ibsen's dramatic strategies behind a screen of unfanciful middle-class and rather provincial drama were decidedly unsettling. Ibsen's conservative opposition was not entirely obtuse

[31] *Electra* in *The Modern Theatre,* ed. Eric Bentley, I (Garden City, N. Y., 1955), 243.

in accusing him of subversiveness, violation of natural action and feeling, and arbitrariness. Shaw was especially right in attributing to Ibsen the use of "irony" and "paradox," which so irritated Ibsen's conservative critics, and of "parable," which apparently confused them. It is ironical and paradoxical, for example, that Mrs. Alving's wrongdoing in *Ghosts* consists of *not* having left her husband and that the rewards of Victorian conformity in the play should prove to be, in her son Oswald's case, softening of the brain. In *Ghosts,* so to speak, the wages of virtue are paresis.

Moreover, Ibsen's "rearrangement of haphazard facts in orderly and intelligent situations," as Shaw puts it, is mordantly ironic when the memorial building erected in memory of the deceased philanderer Mr. Alving burns to the ground. The orphan asylum, besides, is uninsured. The same clerical oaf who had sent the young Mrs. Alving back to her husband in submission to convention many years before had dissuaded her from insuring the building on the grounds that to insure a charitable institution is to evince a sinful lack of trust in the Lord. If ever a playwright before Shaw contrived events for effects of rather diabolical irony while retaining an outward show of verisimilitude, it was Ibsen. In *Ghosts* a "realistic" indictment of society was accomplished with means that actually violated realistic technique. There was almost as much contrivance in *Ghosts* as in the well-made plays of intrigue and emotional forcing that Shaw the critic scorned so heartily that he dismissed their technique in one of his reviews (with reference to the work of the most efficient of the contrivers, Sardou) as sheer "Sardoodledom." The sole difference was that, as Shaw could not fail to observe, Ibsen contrived dramatic events in order to invalidate, rather than support, convention, and in order to achieve irony rather than heroics or sentiment.

It is because this was not at all the case when the most popular Victorian playwright Arthur Wing Pinero wrote a seemingly modern play such as *The Second Mrs. Tanqueray* that Shaw blasted him in a famous review. Pinero contrived to undo the marriage of a Victorian gentleman to a woman with a lurid past by having the man who once had kept her suddenly turn up as her stepdaughter's suitor. Coincidence could not have had a longer arm or a more serviceable one in reassuring a righteous Victorian family that society would not be contaminated in the long run. Poor Paula Tanqueray had to die in the play to prove that, although Pinero was a daring modern playwright in presenting a fallen woman on the stage, he could nevertheless be trusted to conclude that the marriage of a gentleman and a former courtesan could not possibly work out well.

Shaw's most conclusive summation may be given in Shaw's own words in *The Quintessence of Ibsenism,* and these take us, as previously noted, well beyond Ibsen to Shaw himself and to many a latter-day modernist playwright. The technical novelty of the Ibsen and post-Ibsen plays, Shaw concludes, is "first, the introduction of the discussion and its development until it so overspreads and interpenetrates the action that it assimilates it, making play and discussion practically identical"—which is surely the best general definition of drama of ideas. Following this, the summation lists the detailed strategies of the "substitution of a forensic technique of recrimination, disillusion, and penetration through ideals [*sic*] to the truth, with a free use of all the rhetorical and lyrical arts of the orator, the preacher, the pleader, and the rhapsodist." [32]

With Shaw's summary it is possible to define the rationale for this paper as an integral part of a program on "Ideas in the Drama." With his provocative definition of Ibsenism Shaw introduced us to that considerable portion of the modern drama that exemplifies modern social and moral thought, and even philosophy—as in the case of existentialist drama represented by Sartre's *No Exit* and *The Flies.* The so-called ideas could be brought to the surface, as in Shaw's *Don Juan in Hell,* or imbedded in the characters and story, as in his *Saint Joan.* They could come to the surface as an assertion as in Brecht's *Mann ist Mann,* or as a question and challenge, as in the same author's *Good Woman of Setzuan.* They could be given a contemporary content, as in Shaw's *Major Barbara,* or a retrospective, quasi-historical one, as in his *Caesar and Cleopatra.* They could be propounded, as in *Back to Methuselah,* or dallied with, as in that delightful "farce of ideas," *Misalliance.* At times the result has been comedy, at times serious drama—only very rarely tragedy—and quite often a blend of the comic and the serious that constitutes, with the help of irony, as in the case of Friedrich Duerrenmatt's *The Visit,* a genre of modern "dark comedy" concerning which Shaw's declaration is perhaps the most apt: "The jests do not become poorer as they mature into earnest." [33]

[32] *Major Critical Essays,* p. 146.
[33] *Ibid.,* p. 134.

EDWIN A. ENGEL

*Ideas in the Plays of Eugene O'Neill*

Adolescence may be a crucial period of one's life, but in Eugene
O'Neill's case it was virtually his entire life—the single reality,
the source of all nourishment emotional and intellectual. The
plays strongly suggest this, and the recent biographies confirm it.
To the end of his playwriting career O'Neill continuously drew
inspiration from the dozen years beginning about 1900 (when he
was twelve) and extending through 1912. "What haunted, haunting ghosts we are!" he was to have one of his heroes exclaim.
"We dimly remember so much it will take us so many million
years to forget!"[1] He remembered vividly, not dimly, the beginning of his religious apostasy at the turn of the century, the
bitterness toward his father and the evidence that intensified it,
the discovery of his mother's narcotics addiction, the depressing
spectacle of his older brother's spiritual and physical deterioration,
his own chronic drinking, his first mismarriage, his experiences at
sea and as a vagrant, his attempted suicide, his work in the
theater, his bout with tuberculosis, his enthusiasm for the philosophy of Nietzsche. In 1912, while working on the local newspaper, the New London *Telegraph,* O'Neill published some
verses called "The Lay of the Singer's Fall"[2] about an idealistic
boy whose youthful innocent certitude is subverted by the mock-
ing "Devil of Doubt." The last stanza read:

[1] *The Great God Brown* (New York, 1926), Act II, scene 3.
[2] November 27, 1912.

And the lips of the singer were flecked with red
   And torn with a bitter cry,
'When Truth and Love and God are dead
   It is time, full time, to die!'
And the Devil in triumph chuckled low,
   'There is always suicide,
It's the only logical thing I know.'
   —And the life of the singer died.

A remarkable example of adolescent prescience, the poem was an abstract of the themes in the work of O'Neill's mature years.

Also in 1912 appeared evidence of O'Neill's abortive social consciousness, again in verses in the *Telegraph* and subsequently in the New York *Call*. He was to know individual anarchists, socialists, and communists; but by 1921 he rejected all dogma— social, political, and religious. Thereafter he was satisfied with being indignant, at times satirical, about the acquisitive spirit and about materialism generally. For the most part his plays seldom referred to anything topical. In *Strange Interlude*, to be sure, the heroine had been in love with an aviator, and mention was made of hospitalized soldiers. Otherwise the consequences of world war, of war in general, interested O'Neill but little. In *Days without End*, written during the Depression, he showed an awareness of national disaster but expressed contempt rather than compassion for the victims. Thus, he delivered a message through his hero:

I listen to people talking about this universal breakdown we are in and I marvel at their stupid cowardice. It is so obvious that they deliberately cheat themselves because their fear of change won't let them face the truth. They don't want to understand what has happened to them. All they want is to start the merry-go-round of blind greed all over again. They no longer know what they want this country to be, what they want it to become, where they want it to go. It has lost all meaning for them except as a pig-wallow. And so their lives as citizens have no beginnings, no ends. They have lost the ideal of the Land of the Free.[3]

If O'Neill appeared in his plays to have taken only slight interest in current events or to have had little sympathy or hope for suffering humanity, it was partly because of his generally misanthropic outlook, partly because he deliberately concerned himself with timeless matters, partly because he had isolated himself from the external contemporary world by walling himself inside those early years of his life, a "haunted, haunting ghost."

Throughout most of his career O'Neill dealt with big ideas, for he wished to do what he called "big work." Generally avoiding the topical and the transitory, he preferred to treat ideas that are universal and abstract: Man, Life, Death, Love, Hate. The relation between man and man did not interest him at all, he is reported to have said; "I am interested only in the relation between man and God." The duty of the modern playwright, he thought, was "to dig at the roots of the sickness of today," the cause of which was "the death of the old God"[4] and the failure to find a new One. Without God life has no meaning, and the fear

[3] (New York, 1934), Act III, scene 2.
[4] *The Intimate Notebooks of George Jean Nathan* (New York, 1932), p. 180.

of death cannot be comforted. O'Neill dug for some twenty years, mainly at his own roots. Energetically applying himself to the task, he wrote a series of plays that concluded in conversion scenes, scenes whose ecstatic religiosity was simulated, whose fervor was artificially induced. In one play of the series he had his protagonist speak scornfully of his "fixation on old Mama Christianity." [5] There is little doubt that O'Neill was diagnosing his own condition. Had he completed the diagnosis, he would have included his fixation on Mama and Papa O'Neill, on brother Jamie, and on himself. Obsessed with the relationship between himself and his family, he repeatedly returned to the scene of whatever crimes—his family's and his own. Few writers have wrung so much agony and material for so many plays out of their adolescent years.

Before 1922, drawing upon the experiences of his sea, saloon, and sanitarium days, O'Neill had written naturalistic plays in which the simple-minded, insensitive main character became the victim of fate in various forms: psychological (the fixed idea), biological (the primitive past), physical (the sea). During this time and in these plays he occasionally introduced an incongruous figure: the sensitive, brooding, self-pitying, guilt-ridden, life-weary dreamer and, in one instance, inebriate. In *The Hairy Ape* (1922) the insensitive type prevailed, but he represented Man with a capital *M*—individually an ape, collectively the primal horde. With neither a past nor a future, Man could do nothing about the unbearable present. The materialistic world of today further brutalized and frustrated him, while religion and proposals for social and economic reform were beyond his feeble

---

[5] *The Great God Brown,* Act I, scene 1.

ability to understand. He was abysmally ignorant. "Belonging" (O'Neill's word) to nothing, the brute comforted himself by drinking, by drinking and "dope-dreaming."

*The Hairy Ape*—naturalistic in its outlook, expressionistic in its method—was a turning point in O'Neill's playwrighting development. Wasting little pity on the hopeless primal horde, O'Neill next turned to the figure nearer his heart: the life-weary soul who could not belong, even to a world of apes, but who found the apes' prescription for survival—drinking and dope-dreaming—as effective as they had. O'Neill himself had long since been a confirmed inebriate. But alcohol was not entirely a refuge from reality; it also could heighten reality by stimulating the mystical faculties. It is "the great exciter," as William James observed, "of the *Yes* function in man." [6] O'Neill was a nay-sayer by temperament and habit, but he had a predilection for yea-saying and worked at it ardently so long as he was able. Since he was eighteen he had known the work of the most vociferous yea-sayer of them all and at last discovered a way to put Nietzsche to use.

In *The Birth of Tragedy* Nietzsche had perceived two forces operative in Greek tragedy before Euripides. The first of these he identified as Dionysian, its physiological analogue being the state of drunkenness. The other was the Apollonian, whose physiological analogue was dream. As a disciple of Nietzsche, O'Neill thus found a way to dignify his pathological tendencies. Nietzsche had a special appeal for O'Neill, as he had for scores of writers and countless readers in Europe and America during the first two decades of the twentieth century. Among the writers was Strind-

---

[6] *The Varieties of Religious Experience* (New York, 1902), p. 378.

berg, whose temperament and genius were strikingly similar to
Nietzsche's. It was the reading of Strindberg's plays when O'Neill
first started to write in 1913, the Gelbs have reported him as saying, "that, above all else, first gave [him] the vision of what
modern drama could be, and first inspired [him] with the urge to
write for the theatre [himself]." Together, as the Gelbs have said,
Nietzsche and Strindberg were O'Neill's literary heroes and
"became in some ways a pattern for O'Neill's life." [7]

To those in the vanguard of American critics and writers
Nietzsche offered a religion and an aesthetic, a mythology and a
psychology. He provided a formula for such as O'Neill, who had
repudiated both Scripture and Darwinism: substitute Dionysus
for Christ, the satyr for the ape. He not only anticipated Freud;
he helped clear the way for Freudianism. To the artist who
wished to escape from realism he lent support by disparaging the
"naturalistic and inartistic tendency." He offered the doctrine of
Eternal Recurrence, his own version of death and rebirth. And
to those, like O'Neill, who suffered from world-weariness and
life-sickness, he taught struggle in place of resignation, ecstasy in
place of denial. Such was the Dionysian way of life that O'Neill
tried to adopt.

In his effort to resurrect Dionysus, O'Neill had the cooperation
of his friends and associates Kenneth Macgowan and Robert
Edmond Jones, who shared his apocalyptic fervor. The three of
them took charge of the Provincetown Playhouse in 1923. In 1921
Macgowan had published a manifesto called *The Theater of
Tomorrow* that was a plea and a plan for the restoration of the
theater to its original and proper function: a place for the "in-

[7] Arthur and Barbara Gelb, *O'Neill* (New York, 1962), p. 234.

stinctive expression of godhead." "The problem," said Macgowan, "is to find a way for the religious spirit independent of the church," a way to make the theater itself religious. The drama, to achieve this end, must recognize man's identity with the "vast and unmanageable forces which have played through every atom of life since the beginning." Once he recovers his "sense of unity with the dumb, mysterious processes of nature," [8] man once again will belong. Intoxicated by these grandiose conceptions, O'Neill set out to implement them.

He took tentative steps inside the theater of tomorrow when he converted his formula, dream and drunkenness, to vision and rapture, ending his plays in a high pitch of ecstatic affirmation. But not till *Desire under the Elms,* in 1924, did the Dionysian spirit manifest itself. It was at this time, too, that O'Neill began to dig at the roots of his own sickness. His father, mother, and brother had died between 1920 and the composition of *Desire under the Elms.* Imbued with Nietzschean defiance and vitality, he managed to overcome his grief, to affirm life, and to record its "most terrible and most questionable qualities," "declare them good and sanctify them." [9]—all as Nietzsche had directed. Thus O'Neill depicted in *Desire under the Elms* such assorted sins and crimes as greed, lechery, incest, adultery, revenge, and infanticide; he celebrated the triumph of pagan naturalism over indurated religion as well as the victory of mother and son over the father.

This was the first of many plays in which O'Neill presented the discordant unholy trinity of the father, the son, and the

[8] (New York, 1921), pp. 177, 264–65.
[9] *Beyond Good and Evil,* tr. Helen Zimmern (London, 1923), p. 228.

mother—the father usually menacing, the son at odds with him, the mother usually the protective and loving ally of the son. In *Desire under the Elms* Ephraim, the father, was the embodiment of harsh paternity, a religious fanatic, full of sexual prowess and physical strength (although he was seventy-five). He was invincible and indestructible, part Jehovah, part satyr. He was on good terms with all the creatures on his farm except his sons. His young wife, Abbie, was the personification of fecundity and of tender, sinister maternity. Eben, the youngest son, was the victim of maternal deprivation and of the father, who scorned his weakness. By winning Abbie, the son triumphed at last over the father and gained a mother. Unrepentant, except for the crime of infanticide, son and mother-mistress paused, as they were being led off to jail at the end of the play, to kiss, to reaffirm their love, to admire the sunrise, to look up "raptly in attitudes aloof and devout." [10]

If Nietzsche stimulated O'Neill's imagination and helped him to release his inhibitions and write of deeply personal feelings, Freud and Jung illuminated the results. O'Neill knew the work of the analytic psychologists but, in perfect sincerity I think, denied their influence. His position was that of other writers before Freud became known outside his profession, writers of fiction and of drama who concerned themselves with the idea of father-son enmity, mother-son affection. Nevertheless, Freud's speculations on the origins of religion and morality in *Totem and Taboo* (1912, translated 1918) had an interesting relevance to the work of O'Neill. In that study Freud reconstructed the conditions of the primal horde, described a rebellion of the sons against

[10] (New York, 1925), Act III, scene 4.

the violent primal father who stood in the way of their sexual demands and of their desire for power. It was evident to Freud that, after the idea of God appeared, he was "in every case modelled after the father and that our personal relation to god is dependent upon our relation to our physical father, fluctuating and changing with him, and that god at bottom is nothing but an exalted father." The revolt was not of Satan but of the son, who was related to earlier conceptions of a god who had "enjoyed the favors of maternal deities and committed incest with the mother in defiance of the father," [11] finally murdering the latter. In O'Neill's play if the old God—the father—is not yet dead, it is not because the son hadn't tried to kill him.

Eben's repeated plaintive appeal to his Maw was the earliest indication that O'Neill was to enlist the services of the mother in the struggle against the father and against God. In this he was a good, if unconscious, Jungian. For Jung, too, assigned the predominant role in the instinctual and spiritual world to the mother rather than to the father. The mother, he declared, "is the most immediate primordial image." The patient who "seeks to leave the world and to regain the subjectivity of childhood," the universal "secret longing for the maternal depths," "the childish longing for the food-giving mother," [12] the marrying of a woman who resembles the mother, personifications like Mother Earth, Mother Nature, Mother Church—these were all signs to Jung of the presence of a universal wish to enter the mother's womb a second time and be born again.

O'Neill continued under the aegis of Dionysus for two more

[11] (New York, 1938), pp. 919–20, 923.
[12] *Psychology of the Unconscious* (New York, 1949), p. 427.

plays, in the first of which, *The Great God Brown,* he had his heroes once again enjoy the ministrations of the mother. Abbie had been to all purposes an Earth Mother. She had given the son strength to defy God the Father, and now the Earth Mother, Cybel, helped him to fulfill the promise of the Gospels and to comfort his fear of death. Dion Anthony had been at odds not only with his father who, he mockingly said, "imagines he is God the Father," but with himself (out of desperation he had taken to drink), with God, with wife, and with sons. O'Neill began the play as though he intended to reveal the predicament of the American artist, stifled by a Philistine culture; but it became a personal allegory of the ordeal of the playwright himself. It became the lament of the shy, lonely, misunderstood young man, forsaken by his mother when she died and disappointed to find his wife an inadequate substitute. The mother, dominated by her "ogre" of a husband, was remembered by the son for her "purity." She was "stainless and imperishable." The wife, unfortunately, was "oblivious to everything but the means to her end of perpetuating the race" and therefore could offer neither understanding nor protection. The son had suffered his first great shock when he was four years old, after which he became an atheist. His playmate, he explained, had hit him with a stick, destroyed the picture he had drawn in the sand, and laughed when Dion cried. "I had loved and trusted him," said Dion, "and suddenly the good God was disproved in his person and the evil and injustice of Man was born!" [13] Longing to become a child again, Dion could not help but take a dim view of childhood.

Dion Anthony, in whom the "creative pagan acceptance of life"

[13] Act II, scene 3.

was at war with the masochistic, life-denying spirit of Christianity, became a tortured and torturing demonic ironist. Destitute of faith, he was terrified with skepticism. Longing for love—to be loved and protected—he was afraid to love. As death approached, Dion did become a child again. When his *alter ego,* William Brown, was dying, Brown was soothed by the Earth Mother, for he, too, was a sleepy child. A moment later he died, but only after he had experienced an ecstatic mystic insight concerning the Gospels: "Blessed are they that weep, for they shall laugh!" The child entered the kingdom of a heaven that resounds with laughter. The old God who was dead was replaced by a new one conceived in the image of Zarathustra the "godless," he who beseeched the "higher men" to learn how to laugh. As if such joy were not enough, O'Neill also invoked Nietzsche's doctrine of Eternal Recurrence, the "highest formula of affirmation that can ever be attained." "Always spring comes again bearing life!" the Earth Mother intoned. "Always again! . . . life again! summer and fall and death and peace again!" [14]

In *Lazarus Laughed* O'Neill ended his discipleship to Nietzsche, while making his last and most strenuous attempt to write for the Theater of Tomorrow. *Lazarus Laughed* was concerned with the rebirth of Dionysus, its theme being affirmation of life, denial of death. "The fear of death" O'Neill declared to be "the root of all evil." When Lazarus returned from death, his father was delighted to have him reborn to him. Thereafter, scene by scene, Lazarus became progressively younger, eventually to become a child and then to be born again without dying. Friction between father and son soon began when the former, whose

[14] Act IV, scene 2.

God, like Ephraim Cabot's, was Jehovah, cursed the son for being of Jesus' party. When Jesus died, Jew and Christian alike displayed a vengeful fanaticism; and this was the occasion to replace both Jehovah and Christ with Lazarus, whom O'Neill then revealed to be Dionysus, whose prophet was Zarathustra. Zarathustra had preached his sermon, not on the mount but as he descended, exhorting Man, who was "once an ape" and who "remains more of an ape than any of the apes," to surpass himself, to become the Superman—a yea sayer and a laugher. "Laughing have I consecrated!" spake Zarathustra. "Ye higher men, learn, I pray you—to laugh!" [15] This was why Lazarus laughed. And yet he was Nietzsche's Dionysus with a difference. Although he was a yea sayer, a laugher, a lover of eternity, an exemplar of the doctrine of Eternal Recurrence, he was also loving, compassionate, maternal, and full of rapturous other-worldliness. Lazarus was, in short, the masculine counterpart of the Earth Mother and the pagan equivalent of Christ—the Mother and the Son in one person. O'Neill reconstructed everything to fill the heart's need: the conception of the Mother, the philosophy of Nietzsche, the teachings of Freud.

A spiritual epicurean, Lazarus rejected the egoistic belief in the immortality of the soul and argued that death was merely change, that Man must joyfully cooperate with the divine plan by willing his own annihilation. Having identified himself with the Universe, the Universe with himself, Man would belong and cease to be lonely. The tragedy was that he was unable to surpass himself, to accept the religion that Lazarus preached and for

[15] *Thus Spake Zarathustra,* tr. Thomas Common (Edinburgh, 1914), pp. 7, 363.

which he sacrificed himself. Appearing collectively as the Crowd, individually as Caligula (who squatted "monkey-wise" and referred to himself as "a trained ape"),[16] Man remained an ape—neither evil nor important, only despicable.

Although Lazarus was the embodiment of the most essential maternal attributes—comfort and love—he was not the only example of maternity in the play. Miriam, wife of Lazarus, was the counterpart of Dion Anthony's wife, who had been oblivious to everything but the means to her own end, a stubborn singleness of instinct that prevented her from understanding what her husband was getting at. Unable to comprehend that there is no death, Miriam persisted in weeping and mourning for the "dead." The other example of maternity was Livia, mother of Tiberius and the antithesis of Miriam. A sinister, "subtle, and crafty woman," [17] she loved only power and used her son to gain that end. Deprived of tender, maternal love, Tiberius became the most contemptible of men. He not only hated others but loathed himself. Yet he, too, yearned for the innocence and love of early childhood, before he perceived that his mother had never loved him, before his great disillusionment.

After *Lazarus Laughed* O'Neill stopped writing plays for pagans. The rhapsodic quality left his work as the nay saying tendency returned, as the Bacchic reveler became once again the solitary drinker. The change coincided with, but was not caused by, the dissolution of the Macgowan-Jones-O'Neill triumvirate. O'Neill carried on with plays that were diminished in height but increased in length, plays in which he continued to diagnose the

---

[16] *Lazarus Laughed* (New York, 1927), Act II, scene 1.
[17] Act IV, scene 1.

sickness of today without prescribing a Dionysiac—or, indeed, anything more than a sedative. *Strange Interlude* was a case in point. The play was about the heroine's life with father and, only incidentally, about life with husband, lover, and son, despite the fact that these relationships constituted the strange interlude that gave the piece its title. Nina Leeds's childhood relationship with her father was the single reality of her life. No Electra, she simply discovered that such love was enough, a love consisting of comfort, security, and peace. At the end of Act Nine, the interlude ended, she returned to her father's womblike lap, "warm in his love, safe-drifting into sleep." [18]

During the time of the interlude, extending from adolescence to menopause, Nina's experiences were mostly distressing. Here again the father played a significant part, for it had been his selfish meddling that prevented her marriage to a man who was soon to be killed in the war. Her feelings of guilt and of general unfulfillment precipitated the strange experiences that followed. "It was all your fault in the beginning, wasn't it?" Nina said to her father in Act Eight. "You mustn't ever meddle with human lives again." He had destroyed her happiness, made her self-conscious about her wickedness, caused her to punish herself, and had become for her a symbol of death. When she finally married Marsden, she was in effect marrying her father. In so doing she would be wedded to death, a consummation to be wished as devoutly as the above-mentioned childish benefits that she would also recover.

A neurotic, Nina was a portrait of the woman suffering from the sickness of today. As mother, wife, mistress, she combined

[18] (New York, 1928).

attributes of Abbie, Cybel, and Livia; as daughter she was twin sister to Dion Anthony and a portrait of the artist as a young lady. She complained during the long interlude of many things, none of them tragic. Her passion spent, she declined into a gloomy pathos of self-pity. She discovered that happiness is ephemeral and therefore illusory; that words are merely sounds, appearances without realities; that the dead lover had been, after all, a mythical hero, the product of her romantic imagination; and that her search for God was unrewarding. Having rejected the "modern science God" for his indifference to her "misery of death-born-of-birth," she concluded that the mistake had begun "when God was created in a male image"—God the Father— "whose chest thunders with egotism and is too hard for tired heads and thoroughly comfortless." [19]

We should have imagined life as created in the birthpain of God the Mother. Then we would understand why we, Her children, have inherited pain, for we would know that our life's rhythm beats from Her great heart, torn with the agony of love and birth. And we would feel that death meant reunion with Her, a passing back into Her substance, blood of Her blood again, peace of Her peace.[20]

Like Eben Cabot, the hero of *Dynamo,* the next play, longed for his dead mother. But this time an affair with another woman brought not peace but a tormenting sense of guilt. He pleaded "like a little boy": "I don't want to know the truth! I only want

[19] Act II.
[20] *Ibid.*

you to hide me, Mother! Never let me go from you again!" [21]
Henceforth O'Neill was to find a meaning for guilt and sin.
They were associated only with the Mother. On the other hand,
so also were the supreme human needs, love and peace. Love was
mother love, peace was in the womb. The theme of *Mourning
Becomes Electra* was the yearning throughout death-in-life—a life
perverted by the worship of God the Father—for what O'Neill
called "death-birth-peace" [22]—the reward for worshipping God the
Mother. At last he seemed to have found a new God who could
satisfy his requirements. More than that, he contrived to write an
approximation of Greek tragedy, which relied upon the concept
of crime and retribution. Having passed beyond traditional good
and evil he had then to reestablish a moral-religious system. This
he did by basing it upon a matriarchy. If Freud could trace the
beginning of religion and morality to the murder of the primordial father, O'Neill could seek their source in an offense against
the primordial mother. Thus, the calamities that haunted the
house of Mannon were traced to a central primal offense, the
crime against Marie Brantôme, a mother, a crime whose classical
counterpart was that which Atreus committed against his brother.

General Mannon—O'Neill's Agamemnon—had returned from
war, seeking to love his wife and asking that she love him. Far
from sacrificing a daughter, dallying at Appomattox, and bringing back a mistress, the General's only manifest crime had been
the possession of a characteristic Mannon ineptitude where love
was concerned. He was the personification of death-in-life, and

[21] (New York, 1929), Act III, scene 3.
[22] "Working Notes and Extracts from a Fragmentary Work Diary," New
York *Herald Tribune* (November 3, 1931).

his appearance was that of "a statue of an eminent dead man." [23]
He was loved by no one, not even by his daughter Lavinia who,
as Electra, should have behaved more Freudianly. Lavinia was the
jealous rival of her mother, but not for the father's affections. She
sought, rather, to depose the mother in order to succeed her, an
aim that she achieved when her brother murdered the mother's
lover, not to avenge his father's death (he had rejoiced in that)
but in order to have the mother to himself. By killing her lover
he caused her death, after which he suffered the deepest anguish
of guilt. Cooperating with the Furies, Lavinia suggested to him
that he commit suicide. "Yes! That would be justice," he said,
"now you are Mother!" But then he realized that "It's the way to
peace—to find her again—my lost island—Death is an Island of
Peace, too—Mother will be waiting for me there." [24] With the
death of the brother, Lavinia was the last Mannon. She broke the
chain of crime and retribution by remaining unmarried and
living with the dead inside the ancestral home. "It takes the Man-
nons to punish themselves for being born," she said, "with a
strange cruel smile of gloating over the years of self-torture" [25] that
lay ahead. The great crime had been life itself; living had been its
retribution.

In *Lazarus Laughed* O'Neill had tried to deny death. In
*Strange Interlude* he had denied life but comforted his heroine
with recrudescent childishness. In *Mourning Becomes Electra* he
again denied life but let his heroine remain alive for the masochistic pleasure that it gave her. Having long since discharged

[23] "The Hunted," Act III.
[24] "The Haunted," Act III.
[25] *Ibid.,* Act IV.

Dionysus, O'Neill next diminished the role of the Mother, pausing first to write two plays: *Days without End,* in which he went through the motions of returning to the faith that he had left as he entered adolescence; and *Ah, Wilderness!* in which he recalled the summer of 1906, not as it was but as he wished it might have been. Then in *The Iceman Cometh* he returned once again to his past, to 1912. He was prepared to reduce the demands that he had made of religion—love and peace—and that had been supplied by the Mother. Peace alone now sufficed. To pay off the curse of having been born, one punishes himself by remaining alive. To the masochist that is a source of pleasure; but others, like the derelicts in *The Iceman Cometh,* need to anesthetize themselves against the pain of living. Adrift between heaven and hell, they were purgatorial ghosts silently punishing themselves without suffering. For they had rediscovered the old family remedy—drink and dope-dream—and found peace and contentment. But the theme of the play was not how to live. O'Neill had developed that theme in his early plays, when he had dealt with the life-sustaining power of illusion. He was now discovering how to die. Under the illusion that he was not afraid to die, the protagonist waited for death, which could come only after he had surrendered the last illusion. Peace would be his reward.

Whatever became of love? At one time O'Neill tried to speak well of it. Thus, in an early play, he had converted sexual passion into spiritual need and recorded the benefits of tender love between man and woman, recommending it as a way to conquer disease and death. One character had died of unrequited love. Another had claimed to love love. Still another hated men but loved Man. Then love came to be associated exclusively with the mother, love in its purest, most durable form. At last it occurred to one of the later heroes that perhaps in his soul he hated love. And now in *The Iceman Cometh* O'Neill demonstrated not only that truth, justice, and faith are illusory but that love is non-existent, that it is a pipedream. The main business of the play was to unmask love—all forms, including that of the Mother. A destructive pipe dream, love generated shame, guilt, hate, and death.

O'Neill had long been aware of the face behind the mask, of reality behind appearance, but he had never before given more than a furtive glance at the "skull beneath the skin." "Much possessed by death," [26] he had written *Lazarus Laughed,* in which he tried to deny its existence; *Strange Interlude,* in which the heroine's fleeting fear of death was comforted by returning to the peace, protection, and comfort of childhood; and *Mourning Becomes Electra,* in which the son saw death as a return to the Mother and in which the daughter thought of it as a kind of dessert. *The Iceman Cometh* put an end to evasion. O'Neill faced his death at last. Having come to terms with it, he was prepared next to "face his dead," [27] as he put it, and to come to terms with them. They had haunted his plays for the past twenty years. In *Long Day's Journey into Night* he shut himself in with the O'Neill dead, as Lavinia had with the Mannon dead, to display the family skeletons. O'Neill went back to 1912 once more, to show his father as he really was—not God the Father, not an ogre, not the statue of an eminent dead man, but a credible, picturesque,

[26] T. S. Eliot, "Whispers of Immortality," *Collected Poems* (New York, 1936), p. 61.

[27] *Long Day's Journey Into Night* (New Haven, 1956), Dedication.

pitiful human being—and the mother—not God the Mother, not loving and protective, but romantically self-deceived, wistful, weak, childlike, even sinister in her vengefulness and in her efforts to vindicate herself. As she set out early in the morning on her "long day's journey into night," a ghost-like figure slowly disappearing into the fog of morphine addiction, of dope-dream and oblivion, father and sons, filled with dismay, disgust, and guilt, looked on helplessly, comforted only by whisky. "It's as if, in spite of loving us, she hated us!" said Edmund-Eugene. It seemed to him that she took morphine only for its effect, deliberately to create "a bank of fog in which she hides and loses herself. . . to get beyond our reach, to be rid of us, to forget we're alive!" [28] The fog was a symbol of peace, a refuge for those who must escape not only from life but from love. Jamie, the dissolute brother, also mystified O'Neill. The inference was that he drank for the same reason that the mother took narcotics: the defect of love. This was the rock upon which the family had foundered.

During all those years O'Neill had been reliving his adolescent experiences and agonies and had failed to come so close to diagnosing the sickness. His heroes, however much they spoke of loving and strove to love, never convincingly succeeded. For in their childish self-obsession they demanded love only for themselves. Aware of this, O'Neill repudiated it entirely in *The Iceman Cometh*. Then, the following year, in *Long Day's Journey,* he reversed himself, risking the loss of peace for the sake of love —or if not quite love, then its close equivalent: "pity and understanding and forgiveness." [29] He tried to absolve not only himself

[28] *Ibid.,* Act IV.
[29] *Ibid.,* Dedication.

but his family as well. O'Neill culminated both his quest and his career with *Long Day's Journey* and *The Iceman Cometh.* I am convinced that they are not only his finest plays but that they have not been surpassed anywhere since they were written.

He wrote one more play, his very last, and a comparatively feeble one, *A Moon for the Misbegotten*—about the older brother. Approaching the end of his life in 1923, Jamie was tormented with guilt over his feelings about the recently dead mother. Through the love of Josie, an oversize, powerful young woman, he was made at last to feel "at peace with [himself] and this lousy life—as if all [his] sins had been forgiven." Josie started out as if she were going to be the counterpart of Abbie in *Desire under the Elms,* but O'Neill made a special point later in the play of her virginity. She was not only a virgin Earth Mother, she was the Virgin herself, "this big sorrowful woman hugging a haggard-faced, middle-aged drunkard against her breast, as if he were a sick child." [30] The image that O'Neill evoked was that of the Virgin and Child, the *Pietà,* or a combination of the two—a tableau grotesque but not blasphemous. Once again he had come as close to love and pity as he ever had. To be sure, he saw in his brother Jamie his own character and his own plight. That was a reality that at this stage of his career he would not have denied or evaded. If self-love and self-pity were the face behind the mask of love, so be it.

Tormented though he himself was, O'Neill was spared his brother's fate, and that of his sons. His playwriting must have saved him. The theater, which he had once tried to make religious, was a substitute for the Church which he had left and

[30] *A Moon for the Misbegotten* (New York, 1952), Act IV.

served him probably as the Church would have, as a place of refuge rather than of worship. As a poet he tried to "transmute his personal and private agonies into something rich and strange, something universal and impersonal." [31] But succeeding or failing, he used the theater as a vast public confessional, a great therapeutic couch. To be sure, he could not have done that were it not for his impressive talent, his technical skill, his knowledge of the theater. Were it not for that, he, too, would probably have been a derelict or a suicide like the other male members of his family— with the exception of his gifted father.

O'Neill examined his "sickness of today" with monomaniacal concentration and intensity, repeatedly tracing it to the source of infection. This backward tendency was apparent even in the naturalistic early plays. And he himself was conscious of it. One of his characters called it "the cowardly yearning to go back," [32] but back he always went. Whether to cheer himself up or to exercise the artist's prerogative, he transformed family, religion, philosophy, psychology, and pathology (alcoholism, neurotic fixation, inordinate fear of death, terror of skepticism) to fit his personal and dramatic requirements. His intensity of feeling too often had no objective equivalent in the plays. When he strained to communicate what was repressed or what was ineffable, he was often awkward, banal, and prolix. His ambition to do big work in the theater—to surpass his father, some critics think—resulted frequently in something grandiose, turgid, adolescent, even ludicrous. Many of the foregoing features were obscured in produc-

---

[31] T. S. Eliot, "Shakespeare and the Stoicism of Seneca," *Selected Essays* (New York, 1932), p. 117.

[32] *Days Without End,* Act I.

tion, for O'Neill's drama played better than it read, as drama should. But it was not only staging that rescued the plays, nor was it their novelty—experiments with the masks, the asides, and so forth; it was something organic, the product of O'Neill's dramatic imagination and sense of artistic form. I am referring to what O'Neill called the "mystical pattern which manifests itself as an overtone"[33] and which, when it was permitted to do its own work, enriched the play and communicated idea and emotion more effectively than did the language of the piece. The organic presence of symbol and myth—Biblical, pagan, psychological—was one of the very impressive aspects of O'Neill's playwriting. It was best exemplified, I think, by *Desire under the Elms;* but it was effective, too, in *Strange Interlude, Mourning Becomes Electra, The Iceman Cometh* (in which Cyrus Day has discerned interesting Biblical resemblances), and in the Epiphany-like scene of *A Moon for the Misbegotten.* I am referring also to the structure of the plays, a case in point being *Long Day's Journey into Night,* which Eric Bentley has described as

a kind of classical quartet. Here O'Neill eschews the luxury of numerous minor characters, crowds, and a bustle of stage activity. He has a few people and they talk. This has given the public an impression of shapelessness. . . . *Long Day's Journey* is a dramatic achievement which at first glance *seems* formless. Later, one discovers the form. The play has the outward calm and formality—not formlessness!—of French classical tragedies. Like them—and like *The Iceman*—it observes the unities.[34]

[33] The New York *Evening Post* (February 13, 1926).
[34] "Eugene O'Neill," in *Major Writers of America,* ed. Perry Miller (New York, 1962), II, 570.

In the many plays in which O'Neill did not observe the neoclassical unities he achieved form through the cyclic arrangement of the action: the identity of the end and the beginning, the eternal return, the backward tendency. Form and idea were one. And so, too, were art and life. When O'Neill lay dying, he is said to have "clenched his fists, raised himself . . . in his bed and gasped: 'Born in a hotel room—and God damn it—died in a hotel room!' " [35]—a most appropriate epitaph.

[35] Arthur and Barbara Gelb, *O'Neill,* p. 939.

◆§§◆

# Brecht and the Drama of Ideas

When Bertolt Brecht's *Baal* was produced at the Theater in der Josefstadt in Vienna on March 21, 1926, it was preceded by a prologue, written for the occasion by Hugo von Hofmannsthal. Hofmannsthal brings on stage the actors who are about to play *Baal* and puts them through a complicated and esoteric discussion on the importance of the new repertory. His tongue seems to have been lightly in his cheek, because the actors, despite some basic philosophic differences, end in complete agreement as they go off to perform Brecht's play. New repertory, he seems to be suggesting, same old theater. And yet he manages to put into the actors' mouths most of the ideas— most of the clichés, if you like—surrounding the experimental theater of the time. Friedell, for instance, picking up Homolka's suggestion that their period needs saving, defines the villain from which it must be saved: "From the individual. . . . It cannot pull the weight of this prodigious offspring of the sixteenth century which the nineteenth has fattened to its present size." [1]

The implication is that the new theater must have new forms, new intensity, new language to present and to be a part of the modern world in which, as Thimig says, disbelieving his own words, "the individual does not exist any more." What the actors

[1] All quotations from "A Prologue to Brecht's *Baal*," tr. Alfred Schwarz, *Tulane Drama Review*, VI (September, 1961), 111–20. The German title is *Das Theater des Neuen*.

have to say about the disappearing individual are, for the most part, conflicting, contradictory. For Homolka, individuality has become "one of the fantastic embellishments which we have stripped from us," because modern man is involved in a kind of quest, one that seems to be leading him toward a mystic union with the future. It is possible that a distorted view of *Baal* might suggest that it has some connection with such an idea, but the actor's mission sounds nearer the outmoded *avant-garde* which, years earlier, Chekhov smiled at when Treplev gave it his allegiance. Still, the poet's mission was a commonplace of expressionist plays; the transhumanization of the individual is only the reverse of his dehumanization in the face of political or technological forces—a process suggested and resisted in contemporary works such as Karel Capek's *R.U.R.* and Fritz Lang's film *Metropolis*.

None of Hofmannsthal's actors introduce this aspect of the problem directly, but Friedell gets at it obliquely in his discussion of the actor as an amoeba. A side track, one of many in this short prologue, has brought the conversation to a consideration of the ancient problem of the actor, his inability to draw the line between reality and illusion, and Friedell, pretending to speak on that subject, returns to a more general idea when he says: "The actor is the amoeba among all living things and therefore he is symbolic man. The amoeba, that indeterminate primitive creature, which lets the situation dictate whether it should be animal or plant." Once again, the individual disappears, this time to take whatever form circumstances press on him. In still another shift of thought, Friedell reminds his listeners that "the old idea of the two souls inside one breast was also a small rebellion against the dogmatic concept of the Self!" Within a few pages the idea of the individual as some kind of absolute is replaced, explicitly or implicitly, by the individual as a part of or a victim of great forces, as a product of particular situations, as a combination of conflicting elements. All this as a prologue to *Baal*. O my prophetic (if somewhat indeterminate) soul! It might well be used to introduce all of Brecht's work.

When we turn from Hofmannsthal's fictional actors with real names to Bertolt Brecht, the real playwright, or at least to one of his disguises, Brecht the theorist, we hear echoes of the prologue to *Baal*. In his notes to *The Threepenny Opera,* commenting on the attempt of the bourgeois novelist to analyze the individual, Brecht adds, "as though he still existed!" Much that is mystical, haphazard, and slightly comic about Hofmannsthal's philosophic discussion disappears as Brecht begins to theorize in earnest. His self-proclaimed materialism, his pose of cool rationality, his insistence on being a scientific theater man in a scientific age—all these demand a special tone of voice, but still we get the need for a new theater to record the disappearance of the individual. There is no longer a place for the kind of theater, the inheritance from Aristotle, in which the audience is asked to empathize with a hero, to be sucked into the movement of his story, to accept him and his world as inevitable. At a time "when a man must be regarded as the totality of social relationships," as Brecht says in the *Threepenny* notes, "he must be considered as the object of one experiment after another conducted by society." [2] In "A Short Organum for the Theatre," he wrote:

[2] *From the Modern Repertoire, Series One,* ed. Eric Bentley (Denver, Colo., 1949), p. 399. Bentley is presumably the translator.

Undoubtedly a man will respond differently according to his circumstances and his class; if he were living at another time, or in his youth, or on the darker side of life, he would infallibly give a different response, though one still determined by the same factors and like anyone else's response in that position at that time.[3]

Here, again, is symbolic man, the amoeba, and the Epic Theater, so Brecht insisted, was the necessary invention to display, if not to embody, him.

Since Brecht's theory was developed over many years, often in short notes and brief speeches, it is not the neat system that it sometimes appears to be when one summarizes its main points. This is not the place to worry over the internal contradictions of the theory or the occasional conflict between it and the plays. Nor is it necessary here to examine at length the probability that the pre-Epic Theater was a straw man, an invention of Brecht the propagandist, the man who pretended that an audience could only respond to King Lear's anger by sharing it.[4] What I am concerned with in this paper is not the validity of the theory, in either aesthetic or social terms, but that it should have been born out of what is certainly one of the most persistent preoccupations of the theatrical literature of the last hundred years; from Ibsen to Ionesco, the modern playwrights, whatever form of

[3] *Playwrights on Playwriting,* ed. Toby Cole (New York, 1961), p. 87. Tr. John Willett.

[4] Brecht's discussion of Lear can be found in "On the Experimental Theatre," tr. Carl Mueller, in *Theatre in the Twentieth Century,* ed. Robert W. Corrigan (New York, 1963), pp. 94–110.

theater they worked in, have been concerned in some degree, often in great degree, with the uncertain figure of the individual in a face-dissolving society, world, universe. For Brecht this apparent fact of contemporary life fathered a new kind of theater. Its real children, however, are not in the theory but in the plays, for what Brecht considered one of the main causes for Epic Theater's coming into being was actually—and more importantly so far as I am concerned—one of the main subjects of all his plays.

Although one could begin an examination of this Brechtian theme with *Baal,* it might be more useful to start with *A Man's a Man*. It was first produced in 1926, just a few months after the revival of *Baal* that occasioned the Hofmannsthal prologue and not long after Max Reinhardt's third production in three years of a Pirandello play. Brecht, who had apparently attended Reinhardt's rehearsals of *Six Characters in Search of an Author* in 1924 [5] (the year he began writing *A Man's a Man*), was ready by this time to face head on the problem of the individual. *A Man's a Man* is a fable designed to show how personality is an artificial construction of society. It tells how Galy Gay, a gentle and shy porter, sets out one evening to buy a fish for supper and ends as Jeraiah Jip, "the human fighting machine," [6] single-handedly capturing the Sir El Dchowr Mountain Fortress in far Tibet. "A man like that does the turning all on his own," says Jesse

[5] So John Willett reports in *The Theatre of Bertolt Brecht* (Norfolk, Conn., 1959), p. 113.

[6] All quotations from *A Man's a Man* (*Mann Ist Mann*) are from Eric Bentley's translation in *Seven Plays by Bertolt Brecht* (New York, 1961), pp. 69–147.

Mahoney, one of the soldiers responsible for Galy's transformation. "Throw him into a puddle and he'll grow webs between his fingers in two days."

Galy gets thrown into this particular puddle after an accident befalls Jeraiah Jip when he and the other three members of his machine-gun unit attempt to rob the Old Pagoda of the Yellow Monks. Jeraiah's hair gets stuck in a glue trap and part of it is pulled away (that's the play's first transformation). To keep the finger of guilt from pointing at their unit, the other soldiers have to find a hirsute replacement for Jip and, having watched Galy Gay offer to buy a cucumber he does not want, they decide, "this is a man who can't say no." When Jip becomes a prisoner of the Yellow Monks, his temporary replacement has to become a permanent one, what was a masquerade has to become a metamorphosis. Up to this point, the suggestion is that it is Galy's good nature and his stupidity that let the three soldiers work on him. Now, it is self-interest, Uriah's mention of a deal that makes Galy stay with them and deny his wife when she appears. "It's almost as if he was not my husband Galy Gay the porter," she says, "but something quite different, I couldn't exactly say what." The metamorphosis takes place in the long ninth scene, introduced by a direct statement from Widow Begbick unnecessarily explaining what we are about to see illustrated: "You can do with a human being what you will./ Take him apart like a car, rebuild him bit by bit." Galy is induced into selling Widow Begbick a nonexistent elephant (Polly and Uriah wearing a map); he is arrested, tried, executed, and buried. He speaks his own funeral oration, in one of the best identity struggles in the Brecht canon and, in doing so, admits that he is Jeraiah Jip.

Despite the enactment in Scene 9, Galy's metamorphosis is not complete until his longing for his old self is eradicated. It takes the play's other major transformation, that of Bloody Five, to clinch the change in Galy. In the fifth number in the metamorphosis scene, Sergeant Fairchild, "the human typhoon," the terror of the British army, explains how he got the name Bloody Five, but his story is a joke on him since he is wearing a dinner jacket and a bowler hat as he tells it, having been turned into a civilian at a whim of Widow Begbick's. Bloody Five would be the perfect machine soldier if it were not that in rainy weather he "succumbs to terrible attacks of sensuality" and, as Begbick says, "is as undangerous as a milk-tooth." In Scene 10, feeling unmanned by his manhood, Bloody Five is altered, in the technical sense of the word; he castrates himself, so that his natural sexual impulses will not keep him from being his institutional self. Brecht returned to this device twenty-five years later when he adapted J. M. R. Lenz's *Der Hofmeister* for the Berliner Ensemble; the protagonist, who cannot keep his hands off his pupils, castrates himself and, in John Willett's words, "is hailed as the perfect teacher who shall mould the youth of Germany in his own image." [7] Bloody Five's castration is a lesson to Galy certainly, for, having witnessed it, he decides "what a bloody thing it is for a man to be dissatisfied with himself and make such a fuss about his name!" He is ready for the automatistic apotheosis of the last scene.

The metamorphoses of Galy Gay and Bloody Five are not the only transformations in the play. Jeraiah Jip becomes first a god, when Mister Wang decides to make some money out of his

[7] *The Theatre of Bertolt Brecht,* p. 57.

presence in the pagoda, and finally Galy Gay, when Galy, taking pity on him ("I know what a name is worth"), offers him his own unused identification papers. Polly and Uriah become Billy Humph briefly, and the elephant is as real as Galy's desire to make money on it. Since Widow Begbick and her daughters are there to serve the army, they become whatever the occasion demands; thus Begbick can become a customer for an unlikely elephant or she can lie beside Galy, pretending to have slept with him, when his three companions hope that the sight of a woman beside him will convince him he is a soldier. Widow Begbick's kind of pretending, in which the individual is lost in a host of assumed personalities put on to meet the market, turns up often in Brecht's work because there are so many prostitutes among his personae. The prostitute is traditionally as useful an amoeba as the actor. Brecht's most impressive use of this kind of depersonalization comes in *Rise and Fall of the City of Mahagonny* in the duet in which Jenny and Jim make a tentative attempt to get together. The almost sentimental quality of Kurt Weill's music here heightens the effect of her questions, those of a salesman to a buyer: "I have learned, whenever I meet a man, to ask him what he is used to." [8] The scene in *Galileo* in which the astronomer demonstrates his telescope to the city fathers is the same kind of scene, for prostitution is pretty much prostitution wherever you meet it in Brecht.

In *A Man's a Man* the play's theme is evident not only in the characters I have discussed but in summarizing songs and lines, the expected devices of the Brechtian theater. The title song of

[8] Text accompanying recording, Columbia K3L 243, p. 18. Tr. Guy Stern.

the play, which runs all through Scene 9, breaking in at the end
of individual numbers, is a way of saying that Galy's transformation into Jip is not simply an exchange of identities but a movement from the personal to the impersonal; the song, with its
emphasis on the same food, the same girls, the same equipment,
the same death, makes impossible the soldier as an individual.
"Why all the fuss about people?" Jesse asks at one point. "One's
as good as none at all. It's impossible to speak of less than two
hundred at a time."

Although in other Brecht plays it is society in a larger sense
that converts men into functioning ciphers, the army is a good
metaphor to illustrate the process. It is obviously a congenial
one to Brecht because one of his intentions, in *A Man's a Man*
and elsewhere, is to write pacifist satire. His plays have even
more soldiers than prostitutes. A change like that of Galy's is im-
plied in "The Army Song" in *The Threepenny Opera*[9] and in
the corporal's reprimand of the too timid private in *The Caucasian Chalk Circle*. It is illustrated by the SA Man in "The
Chalk Cross," one of the sketches in *The Private Life of the
Master Race,* in which the Parlour-Maid, in her wonder at what
has happened to her sweetheart, is an appalled echo of Galy Gay's
wife: "He's so changed. They've ruined him."[10] The panzer truck
which appears in that play is an image of such a metamorphosis.
The soldiers in it, with their helmets and white faces, are indis-

[9] Eric Bentley has added "The Army Song" to his most recent version
of *A Man's a Man,* but that play, judging by a performance I saw at the
University of Minnesota in August, 1963, is fast becoming as much Bentley
as Brecht.

[10] *The Private Life of the Master Race,* English version by Eric Russell
Bentley (New York, 1944), p. 25.

tinguishable from one another; "They could be puppets," says the
stage direction.[11]

The older son in *Mother Courage and Her Children,* like Galy,
abets in his own transformation; not an efficient quick-change
artist like his mother, he becomes a fighting machine which cannot be put in reverse when peace breaks and so must be destroyed.
Early in that play, the soldier and his mother sing a song in
which a young man, not heeding an old woman's advice, dies the
death of a soldier. The last stage in the depersonalizing process is
to step from the military mask to the facelessness of death. "You
know where it all leads?" Begbick demands of the audience at
*A Man's a Man.* "To death." One of Brecht's earliest and best
statements of this is in the song, "Legend of the Dead Soldier,"
which he used in his second play, *Drums in the Night.* In it the
soldier, who has died a hero's death to get away from the fighting,
is dragged from the grave, declared sound by a medical commis-
sion, enticed with liquor and sex, sanctified by a priest, wel-
comed by the hysterical citizens, and sent on, putrefying, to
pursue his hero's death once more. The suggestion is that the
cheering bystanders, who cannot really see him, cannot see the
dead soldier in every living one.

In such a context, death makes a satisfactory metaphor for the
effacement of the individual. Given Brecht's primarily social and
political orientation, however, one might expect him to get little
use of such a device outside a military setting. Actually, the possibilities must have fascinated him because, even at his most
didactic, in *He Who Says Yes* and *The Measures Taken,* he

[11] *Ibid.,* p. 1. The panzer was added for this version of the play, which
contains 17 of the 24 scenes of *Furcht und Elend des Dritten Reiches.*

adapted death to his own dialectic. Before we consider the special problem of individuality in these *Lehrstücke,* it might be useful to go back and examine the ways the problem was handled in the early Brecht plays other than *A Man's a Man.* In the first of them, *Baal,* death is of major importance. It is Baal's end, the cure of his disease, as the opening song says, and the image of his final defeat. It has been customary, at least among English and American critics, to focus attention on Baal's nihilistic revolt against the world he lives in. Martin Esslin has been able to find in it, or at least in the language that expresses it, "a passionate acceptance of the world in all its sordid grandeur," and Peter Demetz finds a "burning *élan vital*" emerging from "the core of the play." [12] Walter H. Sokel, rejecting such a possibility, sees in Baal's "unending string of debaucheries not an expression of thirst for life but a challenge to and a confirmation of the absurdity of life." [13] If "absurdity of life" here means the impossibility of the individual's making an impression on the world, on the universe, then Sokel's description is a good one, but he goes on to suggest that Baal remains free of organization, and thus he seems to step away from the word *confirmation* in the line quoted above. Not enough attention, it seems to me, is paid to the use of death in this play, for Baal's actions are so hedged in by death that all his protest becomes an illustration of man's inability to hold on to his identity.

It is widely accepted that *Baal* is in part a parody, to use Sokel's

[12] Martin Esslin, *Brecht, the Man and His Work* (Garden City, N.Y., 1960), p. 281. Peter Demetz, "Introduction," in *Brecht, a Collection of Critical Essays,* ed. Peter Demetz (Englewood Cliffs, N.J., 1962), p. 8.

[13] "Introduction," in *An Anthology of German Expressionist Drama,* ed. Walter H. Sokel (New York, 1963), p. xxviii.

words, "of the romantic concept of the poet's martyrdom in the philistine world." [14] But he is more than a joke on a dramatic convention. Although he may be the expressionist poet deromanticized, he has a missionless mission of his own, to make Baal visible in a world of invisible beings. His method is to reject the conventions of success, friendship, love, sex finally—to stand out by standing against. As the play opens, he appears as a poet who refuses publication and critical praise, who would rather affront his would-be friends than accept what they might do to his poetry. At this point he might be any poet refusing to compromise his art in the world of success, but it becomes clear before the play is very far along that Baal's poetry is only a weapon (as in the night club scene in which he enrages and delights his audience) or something to be given or thrown away—an outrage against his own creativity. After all, "poet," too, is a generalizing label.

It is with his appetite and not with his poetic gifts that he makes his chief assault on the world. "One must have teeth," he tells Johanna. "Then love's like biting into an orange when the juice squirts in your teeth." [15] Baal becomes a devourer of women —the characters continually refer to him as an animal—but his insatiability turns his partners into units in a mechanical sexual process. In one scene, two sisters come to him together, but they seem less like participants in an erotic game than like interchangeable parts. "My name is Sophie Barger," says one of his pick-ups, and he answers, "You must forget it." Although Brecht

[14] *Ibid.*, p. xxvi.

[15] All quotations from *Baal*, unless otherwise noted, are from the translation by Eric Bentley and Martin Esslin in Sokel, *An Anthology of German Expressionist Drama*, pp. 305–66.

does not use the metaphor, Baal's bed becomes a kind of assembly line and—as the mechanization literature tells us—the product is no more out of the mass mold than is the man who wields the tool. Baal knows this. It is not the act of sex that is important to him, but his indifference to it; in his postcoital rejection of the women, his refusal to let them sentimentalize the act, he seems to be using cruelty to declare himself. In insisting that his partners be faceless, however, he, too, disappears.

Even his homosexuality, which has been taken as another act of revolt against convention, may be seen as a loss of identity; his love for Ekart suggests in one way the relationship between Garga and Shlink in *In the Swamp,* at least as it is reflected in Garga's drunken musings in the scene in which he calls himself Shlink's woman, an ambiguity of sexual function that makes identity uncertain. Baal's killing of Ekart, which might be seen as a reflection of jealous love for him or, more likely, as an act as accidental and meaningless as the killing in Albert Camus's *The Stranger,* is reduced to conventional banality by the rangers whom Baal overhears discussing it; they assume the crime was committed out of jealousy over the waitress who had been sitting on Ekart's lap. Throughout the play, then, Baal's every effort to proclaim his freedom from a categorizing world is defeated.

At the end of the play, left to die alone, Baal crawls to the door of the cabin and looks at the stars. In a more conventional play this might be taken as a suitable last gesture for the dying poet, one final kick at the universe. Here, however, it is ironic— Brecht kidding a tradition. Early in the play Ekart describes Baal as "a dumpling that will one day leave the sky marked with grease stains." The sky, which Baal speaks much of and which seems to change color to suit his moods, is left unstained by his death. This point is made in the opening song, the "Chorale of the Great Baal," which begins with Baal in "the white womb of his mother" and ends with him in "the dark womb of the earth," while overhead the untouched sky hangs "calm and pallid." The play is filled with images of and statements about death which contribute to the metaphor of Baal's annihilation. In the scene with the dead lumberjack—Baal's attempted outrage of the conventions of mourning—his drunken speech over the dead Teddy has implications for Baal too. "Teddy . . . was a hard worker. Teddy was generous. Teddy was easy to get on with. And of all this, one thing remains: that Teddy *was.*" The reduction of Teddy to the past tense has nothing to do with his conventional virtues, however, and Baal, who disowns them, is en route to the same verb form.

Toward the end of the play, Baal recites "Death in the Forest," in which, at least in the Bentley-Esslin version, these lines appear: "They heard him cry to the darkling sky / And they could see how he clutched that tree / . . . / For he was a man like them all." I can no more find "the darkling sky" than the neat internal rhyme in Brecht's German, but Baal's cry is a continuous one in the play. Baal as a tree-clutcher is seen, by analogy, in the weird scene in the "hospital tavern" in which the Beggar tells the story of the sick man who did not know he was sick, who embraced trees, apparently in an attempt to make contact with something in nature. It is in this scene, too, that we get Googoo's "aria" to Nothing, again presumably a reference to Baal. At the end of that drunken scene, Baal calls Ekart to leave with him, saying: "We'll wash ourselves clean in the river!" Here, however, the suggestion is defacement, not cleansing, for the most persistent image of death in the play is the drowned Johanna, who kills herself after Baal seduces her and about whom he sings Brecht's famous "Concerning a Drowned Girl": [16]

> As her pale body rotted in the river,
> It happened (very slowly) that God forgot her,
> First her face, her hands, at last her hair.
> Then she was carrion with the carrion in the water.

With such an emphasis on death and dissolution in the play, it is not surprising that some critics have found in Baal's vitality a kind of life-wish, but, for me, the play depicts an anarchistic attempt to create personality in a depersonalizing world, and death becomes the metaphor for Baal's failure.

Garga in *In the Swamp* is another of Brecht's heroes trying to make a mark on an unmarkable world. He is more articulate than Baal about what he wants ("a ticket to the Islands"),[17] but he has even less chance of finding the freedom he talks so much about. Where Baal is presumably based in part on Rimbaud, Garga spends much time quoting (or misquoting) the French poet. Garga's is a literary protest—that is, one got from books, not one made through literatures as Baal's in small part is. "We are not free," Garga says, in the soul-baring scene with his mother and then goes on to indicate what he wants to escape from:

[16] The translation is by H. R. Hays, from Bertolt Brecht, *Selected Poems* (New York, 1947), p. 49. The last line of the Bentley-Esslin translation of the poem, "In carrion-carrying rivers she was carrion," seems to me too tricky for the Brecht line.

[17] All quotations from *In the Swamp* (*Im Dickicht der Städte*) from Eric Bentley's translation in *Seven Plays by Bertolt Brecht*, p. 1–68.

all the many other people, all the many good people, all the many other and good people, who stand at their lathes and earn their bread and turn out many good tables for the many good bread-eaters, all the many good table-makers and bread-eaters with their good families.

The only way for Garga to keep from sinking into such other-ness, he believes, is to sail to Tahiti, a land as fictional as Brecht's Chicago and even harder to reach. He never gets on the ship, of course.

Instead, he joins battle with Shlink, who challenges him in the first scene: "*Your* opinion doesn't make any difference either. Only, I want to buy it." It is this struggle—one without motives, if we are to believe the "Author's Foreword"—which robs Garga of the freedom that would give him identity. In the second scene Garga and Shlink change places, and from that point in the play they are little more than conflicting forces in terms of their own struggle, cooperating forces in terms of the destruction they lay about them—of Garga's family, of Shlink's business, of the Salvation Army man. "And I'd still like to see your real face, Shlink," says Garga, "your milk-white, damned invisible face." As though he had a face beyond the one provided by the struggle! At this point I should confess that I have no very clear idea about what Brecht is after in *In the Swamp*. The suggestion of motive, at least on Shlink's part, in the long exchange with Garga in the penultimate scene, almost robs the struggle of its meaninglessness. As a pointless struggle it seems to have more point. It might be tempting—from what we know of the later Brecht—to find some analogy between the Garga-Shlink fight and the competitive struggle of the capitalistic system; not only are there many references in *In the Swamp* to buying and selling, but the struggle there fells innocent victims in the same way, if not in such numbers as the capitalistic conflicts of *Saint Joan of the Stockyards* or *Threepenny Novel*. It is probably more useful to accept the struggle as an unnamed and unnamable process which cannot be avoided.

By the time we get to the last of the Brechtian anarchists, Jimmy Mahoney in *Rise and Fall of the City of Mahagonny*, Brecht had accepted the Marxist interpretation of society. Where Baal and Garga and Shlink are trapped by somewhat indistinct forces, Jimmy is destroyed by very specific ones. He is executed because he cannot pay Widow Begbick for three bottles of whiskey and a curtain rod, which is destroyed in a drunken game of storm-at-sea. Mahagonny, the city that Begbick founds, the "city of nets," [18] is a kind of earthly paradise to which—for a price— men can come to escape the nothingness of the cities in which they live. For Jimmy, however, the permissive Mahagonny is restrictive: "I saw a sign which said / 'Forbidden here!' " His first kick against the system comes in the scene in which his three friends, the lumberjacks who came with him from Alaska, threaten to tie him up until he begins to "act / again like a human being." They mean, of course, until he accepts the comforts of Mahagonny— drink, women, food, rest, the pleasures of nature—the good life, that is, imposed from the outside. "But boys," he says, "I don't want to be a human being." His suggestions for pointless action— that he eat his hat, that he drive to Georgia—are indications of

[18] All quotations from *Rise and Fall of the City of Mahagonny* (*Aufstieg und Fall der Stadt Mahagonny*) tr. Guy Stern. See footnote 8.

the discontent he finally makes specific just before the typhoon is
sighted:

> Oh, with your entire Mahagonny
> not a man will ever be happy,
> because too much peace reigns
> and too much harmony
> and because there is too much
> on which you can depend.

"In this night of horrors," says the Speaker, who introduces
each scene, "a simple woodcutter . . . found the laws of human
happiness." Jimmy, confusing himself with the typhoon, wanting
man to be that kind of force, says: "He must destroy, / whatever
exists." The destruction, it becomes clear as he outlines the new
Mahagonny, is aimed at all rules, all restrictions that stand in a
man's way of doing, of taking whatever he wants. But he infects
his own anarchistic vision when he ends his declaration by saying
to Begbick: "I'll give you money for it." The storm by-passes
Mahagonny. Following Jimmy's suggestion, the city adopts as its
motto, "You may do it," but all that can be done are variations
on what was done before, and these are reduced to the mechanical.
Although such a reduction is implicit in Jake's eating himself to
death, it is shown most specifically in the sex scene, in which
Begbick sits on a raised platform between a man and a girl.
While the chorus sings, "Boys, go faster, / boys, go faster, / boys,
go faster," the lights dim to rise again with the man's chair
empty, only to have it refilled and the routine repeated. Even
Jimmy's adventure at sea is only a drunken invention. The
voyage must end back in Mahagonny where Jimmy is found

guilty of being without money, "the greatest crime, / which exists on the face of the earth." His death is only an illustration of what has been apparent throughout, that his anarchistic bid for freedom was never a possibility in a system in which one is either buyer or bought and in which the system determines the face of both the buyer and the bought.

In the fantasy worlds that Brecht invents to represent the real one, his nihilistic characters have no more luck in holding onto their individuality than do the figures that surround them. The only such person in a Brecht play who does succeed does so in her own fantasy. I mean, of course, the slavey in "Jenny the Pirate," the song from *The Threepenny Opera* in which the girl finally becomes someone by destroying everyone else. Jenny, of course, is not in the play at all; she is only in a song put into the mouth of one of the characters. It is appropriate that the anarchistic impulse should have found so small a corner to hide in in this play, should have "de-faced" itself, so to speak, for with *The Threepenny Opera* we find ourselves in the Brecht world demonstrated in *A Man's a Man,* where a person is only the product of his societal environment. The play's basic assumption is that any relationship between two people—marriage, love, friendship—is necessarily an economic one. That, at least, is *The Threepenny Opera* we get from the notes. A complication arises, I think, over the fact that it is sex, not economics, that brings about Macheath's capture. Brecht attempts to explain this away in the notes by insisting that Macheath's trip to the brothel is not an evidence of impulsive behavior but a matter of habit, a bourgeois Thursday evening out; since he is arrested with women not once but twice, Brecht's discussion on this point seems to say less about the character than it does about the author's intended, and obvious, analogy between Macheath's gang and the bourgeois world. Since the notes came after the play, it is possible that the theorist in Brecht was trying to make them do what the play itself did not quite do—partly because it carried too much of John Gay with it. Still, the London that Brecht presents is an embodiment of Macheath's words in the second-act finale:[19]

> For how can man survive? By simply getting
> Others under, cheating and exploiting all he can.
> He only can survive by sheer forgetting—
> Forgetting that he ever was a man.

Mr. Peachum, "the Beggars' Friend," is the most obvious and most conscious illustration of the truth of the song, but all the other characters, in line and in deed, contribute something to the general idea. When Brecht got around to using the material again, in the *Threepenny Novel* in 1934, he made excessively plain what the notes had declared existed in the glancing satire of the play.

In all of the plays up to this point, Brecht has shown the impossibility of a man's hanging on to an identity peculiarly his own; individuality must be sacrificed to a force greater than man—a force which became specifically environmental as early as *A Man's a Man*. Having adopted Marxism, having found in it new terminology for what was an old situation in his plays, Brecht had also to reject the possibility that the world he presented was

[19] *The Threepenny Opera* (*Die Dreigoschenoper*), tr. Eric Bentley and Desmond Vesey, in *From the Modern Repertoire, Series One*, p. 269.

permanent, inevitable. Greed, envy, cruelty, all these became historical not psychological facts, manifestations of a social order
that, if changed, could let people live differently. Thus, the possibility of change became an important part of the Brecht theory;
one of the main uses of his theater was to be the objective presen-
tation of characters who would be altered if their situations were
changed. The implication of such a theater—one that would help
bring about revolutionary activity—is that man not only could
but must choose. "And I left my own class," Brecht wrote in one
of his poems, "and joined / The common people." [20] The choice,
however, turned out to be between kinds of facelessness. In a
world in which the struggle was between classes, there was still
no room for the individual. This Brecht indicates in the *Lehrstücke* at the end of the twenties.

In the *Baden Lehrstück,* "of Agreement," as the German title
says,[21] the audience is asked to take part in an examination, a
trial, a consideration of right and wrong action. Four flyers—
later identified as one flyer and three mechanics—have crashed
and are asking for water and a pillow. After an investigation
which is designed to prove that man does not help man, aid is
refused the four men, presumably because an act of kindness is
impossible when what is needed is the destruction of the established power structure. The four men are asked to agree with the
decision. In answers to a series of questions, the flyer insists on

[20] From "Verjagt mit gutem Grund." Translated by Martin Esslin, in his
*Brecht,* p. 17.
[21] *Badener Lehrstück vom Einverständnis.* All quotations from Lee
Baxandall's translation, *Baden Lehrstück, Tulane Drama Review,* IV (May,
1960), 118–33.

himself as an individual ("I am Charles Nungesser"); the three
mechanics admit that they are "nobody." The flyer, of course, is
not an individual, but the projection of his function; when his
plane is taken away, his face begins to disintegrate. The Chorus
sings: "Beyond recognition / Are now his features / Begot by him
and us." The mechanics, however, having freed themselves of
self are presumably saved: "But you, you who agree to the flux
of things / Do not sink back into nothingness." Their acquiescence
has been a giving-up to change, to the future, but it is difficult to
see how it is better—for the individual, that is—to be lost in the
historical process than to be lost against it. Given the situation
that initiates the discussion, the image for acquiescence as for refusal is death.

In *He Who Says Yes,* which Brecht based on Arthur Waley's
translation of the nō play *Taniko,* the same agreement to accept
death is presented in a less abstract way. Here, at least, the boy
who allows himself to be thrown over the cliff does so because to
save him the expedition would have to turn back without the
medicine it has set out to bring to the stricken town. Despite the
suggestion of social necessity, however, his acceptance is as obvious
an abnegation of self as that in the *Baden Lehrstück.* It might be
thought that *He Who Says No,* the second version of the play, is
a complete contradiction of the first since the boy decides to live
and convinces his fellow travelers that custom, which demands
his death in this version, must be tested anew with each situation.
In one way, however, both plays show the submergence of the
individual in the group. When the boys throw the victim over
the cliff in *Yes,* they press shoulder to shoulder, each taking part

in the act so that there be "no one guiltier than his neighbor."[22] In *No* they return, again shoulder to shoulder, presumably to face the laughter of the town: "No one more cowardly than his neighbor."

In *The Measures Taken* the problem of acquiescence is again examined, this time in a context that makes very specific the idea that personal identity is impossible in the class struggle. The agitators, who are bringing the Marxist classics to China, don masks before they cross the border. At one level this act is simply a practical precaution—like the assumption of aliases among party workers—a protection for those involved in an illegal and dangerous operation. The words that Brecht gives The Leader, however, indicate that the masks stand for more than that: "One and all of you are nameless and motherless, blank pages on which the revolution writes its instructions."[23] They are, in short, as "nobody" as the mechanics in the *Baden Lehrstück*. The young agitator, however, unable to stand the immediate misery of the people he comes to help, gives way to pity and anger, involves himself in small acts of kindness and of honor; he thus endangers the greater mission, the seeding for the revolution to come. Finally, he rips off his mask, exposes the face that has been exposed symbolically in every act of personal sympathy up to then. Useless to the movement, wounded, a danger to his fellows, he agrees that they should shoot him and throw him into a lime pit, where,

[22] The quotations from *He Who Says Yes* (*Der Jasager*) and *He Who Says No* (*Der Neinsager*) are from Gerhard Nellhaus's translation, "Two Plays," *Accent*, VII (Autumn, 1946), 14–24.

[23] *The Measures Taken* (*Die Massnahme*), tr. Eric Bentley, in *The Modern Theatre*, ed. Eric Bentley, VI (Garden City, N.Y., 1960), 261.

presumably, the lime erases his features once again, and, in death, he sinks back into happy anonymity. Many critics[24] point to this play as a prime example of Brecht's writing something he did not intend to write, a defense of revolutionary tactics that becomes a condemnation. However we might produce the play today, however much the doctrine of acquiescence sounds to us like Mother Courage's song "The Great Capitulation," however much we may want to think of the play as an expression of the poet's subconscious rejection of what he rationally accepted, it is important to remember that Brecht meant it as a positive state- ment. Even the proposed method of production contributes to the idea. The cast consists of four performers who step in and out of various roles, demonstrating what has happened for the Con- trol Chorus which must pronounce a verdict on the action; in his notes to the play, Brecht suggests that the performers take turns, scene by scene, at playing the young agitator. According to Brecht's alienation theory no actor is supposed to become the character he plays, but here, as in all the *Lehrstücke,* there is not even an identification between performer and role. Sometimes one performer, sometimes another fills a particular role; some- times a chorus speaks for an individual. In such a play—even in *The Horatians and the Curatians,* in which acquiescence is not the subject—the form as much as the content demonstrates to the performers and to the audience the virtues of burying the self in the group.

In the other plays of the early thirties, those written before and

[24] Esslin, *Brecht,* p. 296. Walter H. Sokel, "Brecht's Split Characters and His Sense of the Tragic," in Demetz, *Brecht,* p. 133. Hannah Arendt, "The Poet Bertolt Brecht," in Demetz, *Brecht,* p. 44.

immediately after Brecht's exile from Germany—plays less abstract but no less didactic than the *Lehrstücke*—Brecht continued to be involved with the problem of choice. In *The Mother* the heroine at first reluctantly, at last wholeheartedly allies herself with the revolution. In *Saint Joan of the Stockyards* the heroine fails the revolution because she is not quite able to free herself from her class—represented by the Black Straw Hats, the Salvation-Army type of religious group to which she belongs. Although the idea is not presented as clearly as it is in the *Lehrstücke*, it is apparent that what is required of Pelagea Vlassova and demanded of Joan Dark is the sinking of the individual into the movement. This is particularly clear in *Saint Joan* where the workers, except those in Scene 4 who consent to the system to survive, are always indistinct—crowds or voices or undifferentiated worker heroes. The same thing is implicit in *The Mother*, judging by Brecht's complaint about the 1933 production in New York in which realistic staging reduced his Pelagea from a kind of mother to the masses to an ordinary working woman.[25] In his two anti-Nazi plays, *Round Heads, Peak Heads* and *The Private Life of the Master Race*, Brecht examines the consequences of the wrong choice to a people that chooses to see itself racially or nationally rather than in terms of class differences. In *Round Heads, Peak Heads*, the ruler of Yahoo, faced with revolution, abdicates his power to Iberin, who solves the internal conflict by preaching the racial superiority of the Czuchs (the Roundheads) to the Czichs (the Peakheads). At the end, Callas, who had abandoned the

[25] There is a brief discussion of the American production and Brecht's reaction to it in Morgan Y. Himelstein, *Drama Was a Weapon* (New Brunswick, N. J., 1963), pp. 65–66.

revolution to live by his round head, learns the truth of a fellow tenant's assertion: "Czuch or Czich, a landlord is a landlord." [26] The knowledge comes late, for the rebellion is broken, and the country is on the way to a new group identification, the kind that is brought by war. This we see in *The Private Life of the Master Race,* in which the individual scenes indicate the way in which the people of Germany consent to the course that brings them to the facelessness of the panzer group.

In these plays, for the most part, the problem of the individual is only a tangential consideration, implicit in the assumption that he disappears, for good or ill, whatever his political choice. In *Saint Joan of the Stockyards,* however, and with less effectiveness in *Round Heads, Peak Heads* Brecht makes use of a familiar theatrical device to comment on the mechanics of identity. When Joan drives the meat packers out of the Black Straw Hat shelter, and their money goes with them, she is disowned by the organization, stripped of her uniform. The scene is a twisted reworking of the end of Act II of *Major Barbara* where Barbara removes her insignia, just as an earlier identity scene (Joan's recognition of Mauler) is a parody of Joan's meeting with the Dauphin in Shaw's *Saint Joan.* But Brecht has more in mind than kidding Shaw, whose two plays obviously gave much to this one of Brecht's. Joan's uniform is more important finally than Barbara's. In the last scene, after her death, Joan is dressed again as a Black Straw Hat, a bit of business that indicates how the meat packers will turn her into a capitalist martyr but that also reminds us that Joan failed because she never really got out of that uniform. Here

---

[26] *Round Heads, Peak Heads (Die Rundköpfe und die Spitzköpfe),* tr. N. Goold-Verschoyle, *International Literature,* No. 5 (1937), p. 18.

Brecht makes effective use of costume—in the double sense of both uniform and disguise. In the Prologue to *Round Heads, Peak Heads* the Stage Manager explains (one might almost say *explains away*) the play by having the actors exhibit scales, on one of which round heads are weighed against peak heads, on the other fine clothes against ragged ones; the actors introduce their characters in terms of head shape and costume.

Brecht used costume in the same way in *A Man's a Man*, where the chief transformations are preceded by changes of clothes, and in *The Threepenny Opera*, where Peachum outfits the beggars. The usage in *Saint Joan*, however, is particularly important because it seems to be looking toward the last plays where Brecht returns to a direct consideration of the impossibility of the individual and where he makes much of the putting on and taking off of clothes. In *Mother Courage* Kattrin tries on the camp follower's red boots, and the Chaplain changes his costume as often as Courage changes her flag. In *The Good Woman of Setzuan* it is a costume change that indicates the shift from Shen Te to Shui Ta. In *The Trial of Lucullus* the general must take off "his splendid helmet" [27] before he can get through the gate of death. In *The Caucasian Chalk Circle* much is made of the governor's wife's wardrobe, of the fineness of the baby's linen, and, most important, of the judge's robe which Azdak is forever getting in and out of. The finest costume scene in all of Brecht's plays, however, is the one in *Galileo* in which Urban VIII is being dressed; at the beginning he is Barberini, a scientist and Galileo's friend; by the end he is the Pope and consents to the Inquisition's ex-

[27] *The Trial of Lucullus* (*Das Verhör des Lukullus*), tr. H. R. Hays, (New York, 1943). The volume is unpaged.

amining Galileo. The scene is the more effective for the presence
in the play of the April Fools' Day scene with its masquerade
figures and the party scene in which Barberini and Cardinal
Bellarmin wear masks, the one of a dove, the other of a lamb.

In these later plays Brecht has returned to the problem of
identity in a way that recalls his early plays. Once again he deals
with characters who try and fail to be themselves in a world
which demands that they be something else. The basic assumption
here seems to be that there is an identifiable self which must be
buried in the image of man dictated by his function and his class.
The struggle between the two selves, the conflict at the heart of
all these plays, is seen in embryo in Galy Gay's oration over his
own grave, but it is Tiger Brown in *The Threepenny Opera* who
most obviously points toward the protagonists of the later plays.
Brecht makes it clear in his notes that Brown has within him two
different people, "the private citizen and the official," [28] and his
insistence on the genuineness of Brown's affection for Macheath
suggests that the unofficial Brown is very like the natural, the
instinctively good selves that regularly lose out in the later plays.
Although this conception of Brown is only suggested in the play,
the specificity of the notes forms Brown as he appears in *Threepenny Novel,* where Brecht has the space to show Brown's
double nature. Anna-Anna of *The Seven Deadly Sins of the
Lower Middle Class* is another early example of Brecht's use of
split character; in this ballet libretto, the natural Anna (the
dancer) must accept the wisdom of the rational Anna (the singer)
and lose herself in what her family expects of her. A less obvious
early example is Pierpont Mauler in *Saint Joan.* It is possible to

[28] *From the Modern Repertoire, Series One,* p. 396.

see him simply as a caricature of the rapacious capitalist, but the play is more interesting if his bombastic speeches about his longing to be kind are taken not as hypocritical cant but as expressions of a self which his capitalistic function forbids.

These are the predecessors of the divided characters in the last plays. Of Galileo, a great scientist whose self-indulgence finally makes him recant his findings, reduces him to a product of and contributor to the *status quo*. Of Mother Courage in whom the mother is regularly lost in the business woman. Of Lucullus, the man whose small personal pleasures were responsible for introducing the cherry tree into Italy but who is effectively buried in the great general. Of Shen Te, the good woman of Setzuan, who can only survive by becoming Shui Ta, her cold and cruel cousin. Of Herr Puntila, whose goodness when he is drunk disappears with soberness, for a landlord can only be an exploiter. Some of these characters—particularly Galileo and Courage—have outgrown their plays, have suggested to some critics and some audiences a testimony to the human spirit that is not implicit in the play itself.

Only in *The Caucasian Chalk Circle,* in the naïveté of Grusha and the cunning of Azdak, does the natural self seem to be able to out-smart or out-dumb society's pigeon-holing of personality, and this play is a fable of long ago, and it ends with Azdak's disappearing forever. Even so, there is a kind of comfort for all of us in a figure like Azdak, at once the worst and best of men, for the play seems to suggest the possibility of both the selves surviving, which the other plays do not. After all, Azdak wears his own tattered underwear under the borrowed judge's robe. It is a survival, then, but one Brecht described much earlier when he said of Tiger Brown: "and this is not a schism *in spite of* which he lives, but one *by* which he lives." [29] We end then where we began. The individual can only survive in our world by recognizing that he is a psychological pastiche, a gathering of responses to particular situations; the individual can only survive by accepting that he is not an individual.

[29] *Ibid.*

VICTOR BROMBERT

**❧**

# *Sartre and the Drama of Ensnarement*

Tout est piège. *Huis-Clos*

Sartre, whose central concern is man's freedom, seems almost obsessively drawn to a literature of imprisonment. Man's metaphysical freedom is for him the frightening secret of the gods, that secret which Zeus, in *Les Mouches* (*The Flies*),[1] is so reluctant to share with Orestes. And the function of the writer, much like the compulsion of Orestes in the play, is to proclaim this terrifying and exhilarating truth. In his essay *What is Literature?*, Sartre sets forth this function in explicit terms: "The writer, a free man writing for free men, has only one subject: freedom." Yet in that same essay, he calls for a new dramaturgy of *situations,* which he conceives in fact as a theater of entrapment: "Each situation is a trap, there are walls everywhere." [2]

The very titles of so many of Sartre's works—*Le Mur* (*The Wall*), *Huis-Clos* (*No Exit*), *La Chambre* (*The Room*), *Les Séquestrés d'Altona* (*The Prisoners of Altona*), *Intimité, L'Engrenage* (*In the Mesh*), *Les Jeux sont faits* (*The Chips Are Down*)—betray metaphorically an obsession with images of con-

---

[1] After the first reference in the text to any of Sartre's works, the title of the published English translation is given. Quotations from Sartre's works have been translated from the French original by the author.

[2] *Situations II* (Paris, 1948), pp. 112, 313.

finement, enclosure, and immurement. They communicate a sense of the walled-in quality of human consciousness and human existence. Bounded by external contingencies or by the imperatives of a dilemma, the Sartrean hero often appears inextricably jammed-in.

Literal prisons, or places of detention, occur repeatedly in his works. The setting of *Huis-Clos* is a cell-like room, symbol of the living hell of guilt and ceaseless judgment. In this peculiar torture chamber there are no racks: the conventional torture instruments are absent. But there are the atrocious tortures of the mind as it is ensnared by itself and by the relentless glance of the "others"—tortures symbolized by permanent exposure to light, total absence of sleep, and eternal cohabitation with inmates who are also one's torturers. *"Fait comme un rat"* (trapped like a rat), concludes one of the characters. And on one level, the trap is the very prison of a past life that now—since it has been completely lived out—rigidly immobilizes the dead. In *Morts sans sépulture* (*The Victors*) the action takes place in a room where Resistance fighters, while listening to the cries of their comrades, wait for their turn to be tortured. Fear and pride, as well as the distance separating those who have been tortured from those who have been spared, here create prisons within a prison. And in *Le Mur* we witness the anguished night of a political prisoner, during the Spanish Civil War, waiting with other jailed men for dawn and the moment of execution. The cruel tricks of the imagination, the hallucinations and the visceral reactions provoked by fear, the sense of alienation and absurdity as the proximity of death already separates man from his life have perhaps never been treated more vividly—not even by Leonid Andreev, whose *The Seven Who Were Hanged* may well have inspired Sartre.

Even when the setting is not a jail, there are in Sartre's works numerous scenes of confinement. Claustration, in one form or another, is frequently the central motif. Hugo, the young revolutionary intellectual in *Les Mains sales* (*Dirty Hands*), seeks refuge with Olga and remains throughout the play, until his final choice, in what could be termed "protective custody." The prostitute's room in *La Putain respectueuse* (*The Respectful Prostitute*) is also—for a while at least—an asylum for the hunted Negro. At times enclosure is self-imposed. Frantz von Gerlach, the guilt-ridden former German army officer in *Les Séquestrés d'Altona,* withdraws into self-inflicted confinement, complicated by an incestuous relationship with his sister that further entraps him. The bolted door, the walled-up window are symbols of a refusal of life and truth, of a hopeless escape from a bad conscience, which ironically provides further deceptions, as the protagonist flirts with his own delirium. As for "La Chambre," one of Sartre's most successful short stories, it describes a woman's self-imposed imprisonment with her mentally ill husband who slowly sinks into total insanity. Here also the author creates a sense of a prison within a prison. Eve tries in vain to reach her husband beyond the steadily thickening wall of his madness.

Sometimes, notably in *Les Mains sales,* the dramatic structure of the play locks the situation within itself, apparently allowing the protagonist no escape whatsoever. Hugo, who has just been released from a real prison, is hunted down by fellow revolutionaries who have decided to liquidate him. When the play begins, Hugo is given a last chance. In a closed room he is to explain to Olga the motives for his ambiguous murder of Hoederer. The major part of the play is thus a flashback between a suspenseful beginning and an outcome (life or death) that will entirely depend on the answer this retrospective examination of motives will provide. It is difficult to conceive a more immobilizing situation than the one achieved through this dramatic compression of time and irrevocable action within a "theatrical" time (from 9 P.M. to midnight) that barely exceeds the actual time of the performance.

The theater, to be sure, lends itself to the prison image. The epic form—whether in the classical epic or in modern fiction—allows and even calls for movement in time and space. Tragedy, especially in the French tradition with its "unities," most often focuses on a crisis in which the protagonists have reached a seeming impasse. Racine's antechambers are not so different from Sartre's cell where characters are locked together in a death dance. And one could easily show that Greek tragedy is filled with images of restriction and confinement: the chains of Prometheus, the fatal webs and nets in *Agamemnon,* the meshes of fate and the trap of intellect in *Oedipus.* The modern stage, with its three walls—the fourth wall being the inexorable eye of the public—may be said to symbolize an issueless situation.

These are no doubt permanent features of the tragic theater. But in Sartre's plays, the prison motif is closely bound up with psychological obsessions as well as with philosophical themes. The flashback, for which Sartre has so marked a predilection, may appear, as in *Les Mains sales,* as a melodramatic rather than a tragic device: it immobilizes a past that seemingly cannot be altered. Yet this is a misreading of the play. The real suspense is not to be summed up by the question: What will happen to Hugo? but by the far more important one: How will he choose to give a meaning to his past act? For it is up to him to bestow a meaning upon it. The flashback thus leads not to a sterile investigation but to a choice and consequently to an act *in the present*. The element of surprise—for there is a *coup de théâtre*—is not at all related to Hugo's fate but to his will and to his decision. And the *coup de théâtre* is the hero's breaking out from the imprisonment of what appears like a set, prearranged order.[3] The philosophical implications of such a breaking out are clear. The significance of a human act must not be sought in motivation, which is always muddled, nor in the prison of a given psychology, but in the allegiance to the act itself—for man *is* his acts—and in the meaning man imposes in relation to a present situation. Every heartbeat thrusts into the world a decision through which we reinvent ourselves. When Hugo, at the end of the play, kicks open the door so his murderers can come in, he paradoxically escapes to an authentic freedom.

Sartre's own favorite haunts, as well as the *luoghi ameni* of his poetic universe, are most often both anonymous and walled-in: hotel rooms, dimly lit cafés, night clubs (the French *boîte de nuit* evokes the sealed-in atmosphere), reading rooms in public libraries—all suggest airlessness and reclusion. Camus' work also provides striking illustrations of this *lyrisme cellulaire*: in *L'Etranger* the stranger Meursault in his North African jail, in "Le Renégat" the renegade in the ghastly chambers of the city of salt, in *La Chute* Clamence sitting out his life in the dingy bar surrounded by the concentric canals of Amsterdam like so

---

[3] Jacques Guicharnaud very aptly observes this tendency on the part of characters to reject the tyranny of a scenario written in advance. *Modern French Theater* (New Haven, 1961), p. 142.

many circles of hell, an entire city locked in and isolated in *La Peste*. Modern literature from Dostoyevsky's underground man to Beckett's pariahs is filled with lonely and hedged-in figures. It is also filled, since *The House of the Dead,* with penal colonies.

The literary historian with a penchant for political or sociological interpretations might be tempted to generalize about the possible relationship between this cellular lyricism and the collective political and ideological tragedies of our time. Sartre himself has been fully aware that his generation was brutally thrust into the nightmare of history. "We were driven to create a literature of historicity," he explains in an essay on the function of literature.[4] Sartre's generation had indeed learned that this was no longer a time to toy with aesthetic problems or to seek private salvation through art—that private salvation was no longer possible, that man was involved in a collective tragedy, and that the very meaning of traditional Humanism was being seriously challenged. The era of concentration camps (*l'ère concentrationnaire,* as it came to be called) reminded the writer that even imprisonment was no longer a private affair. And the concentration camp has haunted the imagination of Sartre ever since the days of the Occupation. This, too, was a lesson in loneliness and solidarity: a period of humiliation and betrayal, a period when deportation, execution of hostages, and torture became a daily reality, when almost daily man was cornered, exposed to extreme situations and extreme choices between heroism and abjection, when moral problems could no longer be comfortably relegated to the classroom but had to be faced, here and now, leaving little room for cozy innocence. It is significant that the most haunting memory

[4] *Situations II,* p. 245.

associated with the guilty past of Frantz, in *Les Séquestrés d'Altona,* is the construction of a concentration camp on family land sold by his father to Himmler.

This fear of a complicity with evil explains in part why Sartre permanently seeks a complicity with the victims. To be *"dans le coup,"* to be *"dans le bain"* are typical expressions of solidarity, pointing to an involvement and an entrapment with others. They are the social and political equivalent of the metaphysical *"nous sommes embarqués"* of Pascal who, incidentally, also viewed the human condition as a form of collective imprisonment: men in chains, all condemned to die, some of them each day slaughtered in full view of the others. In the eyes of Sartre's generation man must not prefer his private cell to the bitter realities of collective imprisonment. This urge to "be with," this compulsion to enter into a collective prison, has been given its most articulate allegorical form in *Les Mouches* where the inhabitants of Argos are seen as the prisoners of a tyrannized city—prisoners who are, however, willfully blind in the face of their servitude and whose bad faith and secret shame further subjugate them. It will be Orestes' function to carry a lesson of freedom to the inhabitants of Argos. This, however, he will not be able to do unless he himself first becomes a member of the imprisoned community.

The paradoxes, or even contradictions, are apparent enough. How is one to reconcile the self-willed immurement (whose major symptom is incommunicability) with the shame of this private prison and the urge to assume one's role in a collective imprisonment and eventually in a collective liberation? And how are these problems in turn related to the prison metaphor as a structural device whereby the philosopher-playwright stresses the existential responsibility of his protaganists? Or are these problems merely brought together by the coincidence of a persistent prison imagery?

For an answer we may well turn to the one play that, better than any other work of Sartre, dramatizes man's basic dilemma in existential terms—*Huis-Clos*. This play provides a striking illustration of man's double imprisonment: in the self, and through the presence of others. For it is based entirely on a reversed metaphor: it is not hell that is here described as a condemnation to the self under the judging eye of another consciousness, but it is life-in-the-self and in the presence of others that is hell. What the play provides is a figuration of man's simultaneous solipsistic and interdependent condition. *"L'Enfer c'est les autres,"* remarks one of the characters. And, significantly, the original title of the play was *Les Autres*. Every character in *Huis-Clos* is trapped in a private world of guilt and shame: the infanticide, the sexual pervert, the coward. They desperately search for a key to innocence and attempt to break out of their confining cell. In the mirrorless room they turn to the "others" as to consoling or flattering mirrors, only to come face to face with their severe glance and cruel judgment. Through what amounts to psychological *voyeurisme* the other becomes at the same time accomplice, witness, and judge, as mutual confessions turn out to be mere pretexts for exercises in bad faith. The eye of the other is woefully needed, but it is also feared. For man's very identity depends on the presence of a mirror. But the mirror allows for no escape. The search for an exit carries its own paradox: one cannot break through a mirror. The protagonists are thrown back within their own limits, as the much wanted other becomes an object of hate.

What salvation in this hellish trap? *"Regarder en soi"* (to look into oneself), says Garcin. But this is intolerable, and moreover impossible. For man will necessarily recreate within himself a glance that will substitute the glance of the others, he will interiorize a judgment that will play out the hypothetical judgment of another consciousness. Man is caught. The play symbolically comes to an end with an attempt at an impossible murder. There is no solution but to get on with it. *"Lasciate ogni speranza. . . ."* The fellow inmates are bound to each other forever. Solitary and —whether they like it or not—solidary.

Man is thus, in the Sartrean context, condemned to an inalienable subjectivity from which he cannot extricate himself. Contingent and superfluous, his existence is frequently described through images suggesting viscous, gummous, sticky sensations— *"glu"* and *"englué"* are favorite terms in the Sartrean vocabulary. This adhesion to one's own existence is like the awareness of one's own insipid taste. It is also the fundamental cause of man's anguish. For anguish, abandon, and sweating of blood, explains Sartre in one of his essays, begins when man no longer has any witness but himself. "Then he must drink the bitter cup to the dregs, and experience fully his human condition." [5] And it is more than just anguish. It is like a permanent awareness of guilt: the awareness of the original guilt of being. This "sin of existing" described by Roquentin in *La Nausée* (*Nausea*) is shared by almost all of Sartre's characters who, like Brunet in *Les Chemins de la liberté* (*The Roads to Freedom*), feel "vaguely guilty"— guilty "of being alone, guilty of thinking and living. Guilty of not being dead."

[5] *Situations II*, p. 250.

This psychological rift within the prison of self has its philosophical counterpart in Sartre's notion of the irreconcilable, and
at the same time interdependent, relationship of the *en-soi* and the
*pour-soi.* All experience is thus conceived as bipolarized. In his
major philosophical work, *L'Etre et le Néant (Being and Nothingness),* Sartre, in discussing the stumbling block of solipsism,
stresses the double alienation of man, both in relation to the other
and in relation to himself.[6] The Sartrean hero is thus subjected
to an eye—the eye of the other, but first the eye of his *pour-soi*—
before he can attain identity. Stendhal once wistfully complained
that the eye cannot see itself. This is a blessing Sartre does not
grant his characters. To make their suffering greater, it would
seem that they are endowed with precisely such an introverted
vision.

The self-torturing potential of the mind and the self-punishing
workings of the intellect are permanent themes in Sartre's work.
Garcin, in *Huis-Clos,* cries out: "Give me rather a hundred burns
and flayings than this agony of mind." Mathieu, in *L'Age de
raison (Age of Reason),* sees himself rotten to the core:
"Thoughts, thoughts on thoughts, thoughts on thoughts of
thoughts; he was transparent to infinity." Hugo, the young bourgeois intellectual who has joined the revolutionaries in *Les Mains
sales,* knows that he remains trapped and paralyzed by his intellect. He has chosen Raskolnikov as a battle name. The choice is
symbolic: the name Raskolnikov in Russian implies a rift. And
this is true of all of Sartre's intellectuals—and who among his
characters is not an intellectual?—all of them compulsive thinkers

[6] *L'Etre et le Néant* (Paris, 1943), p. 277.

ensnared by the mirror-disease of thought. Sartre's imagery often
suggests a "third degree" type of lucidity: the burning light in
*Huis-Clos,* and in *L'Age de raison* the relentless sun in the
"lucid sky" dazzling Mathieu and forcing him to blink. The
characters of Sartre not only think, they watch themselves think.
Their thoughts are reflected and infinitely multiplied in a looking-
glass that turns into an instrument of self-torture. And there is no
end to it. "Nausea," among other things, is the loathsome weari-
ness that accompanies this pathological cerebration. Consciousness
can find no escape from itself. One is reminded here of Baude-
laire's self-torturer, "L'Héautontimorouménos."

*Huis-Clos* illustrates how this rift within the self is further
complicated by intolerable relations with the others. Sartre's
heroes are prisoners without privacy. And they are caught in an
insoluble dilemma: the need for a witness is closely linked with
the fear of the judging eye. Thus, in *Les Séquestrés d'Altona*
Johanna describes all the members of the family as "jailer-slaves."
And Frantz, who at one point says to Johanna: "I will not let
myself be judged by my younger brother's wife," later pleads
with her to judge him. In the novels there are countless examples
of characters fenced about by the other's consciousness at the very
moment they seem most withdrawn in themselves. Mathieu,
walking through the streets of Paris, suddenly stops aghast: "He
was not alone; Marcelle had not let him go. She was thinking
of him. She was thinking: dirty bastard. . . . The consciousness
of Marcelle remained somewhere out there. . . . It was unbearable to be thus judged, hated." Or this other moment of panic:
"Behind him, in a green room, a little consciousness filled with

hate was rejecting him." [7] The desire to break through the immurement becomes doubly urgent: the other not only judges us, but refuses us and rejects us.

For almost as basic as the guilt of *being* is the sin of *being another*. The bitter and anguished exclamation of Goetz in *Le Diable et le bon Dieu* (*The Devil and the Good Lord*)—"You are not me, it is unbearable"—is echoed throughout Sartre's writings. It reflects a psychological obsession that is closely bound up with a guilt of class consciousness, namely the shame of being a *fils de bourgeois* that has so persistently haunted the French intelligentsia ever since the middle of the nineteenth century and that the writers of Sartre's generation have felt with particular acuteness. It is indeed noteworthy how often Sartre refers to the condition of bourgeois as a form of imprisonment. In *Situations II* he explains that the bourgeois writers are trapped: "Born of bourgeois parents, read and paid by the bourgeoisie, they will have to remain bourgeois, for the bourgeoisie, like a prison, has sealed them in." The proletariat is doubly inaccessible to the bourgeois revolutionary who yearns to reach out to it and be accepted, for it too is trapped in its own class consciousness. It is, explains Sartre in *What is Literature?*, "encircled by a propaganda which isolates it; it is like a secret society, without doors or windows." [8] Ashamed of his own class, Sartre comes to envy those who, according to him, were born prisoners of a more enviable class. How many of Sartre's protagonists share this sense of alienation! Hugo, in *Les Mains sales,* is a typical déclassé who cannot, however, slough off his *"peau de bourgeois."* Goetz, in *Le Diable*

---

[7] *L'Age de raison* (Paris, 1945), p. 23.

[8] *Situations II*, pp. 155, 277.

*et le bon Dieu,* is similarly—though on a more grandiose scale—locked up in his own social condition: a bastard nobleman who cannot become a plebeian. Nasty, the leader of the mob, explains that Goetz cannot save the poor, only corrupt them. And when Goetz desperately proclaims his solidarity ("I am one of you"), Nasty opposes with a flat "No." What right has Nasty to speak in behalf of the peasants? The answer is equally clear: "I am one of them." And Goetz will never be.

But "they" signifies not merely a social group or a political party. "They" are all those who have undergone what I did not undergo, all those who have suffered what I have not suffered. Between their suffering and myself lies all the distance that separates us. Their very imprisonment confines me and excludes me. This separation created by suffering is perhaps the most important tragic theme in Sartre's work. It is at the very core, for instance, of *Morts sans sépulture,* a play whose brutality shocked and disconcerted the audience. But *Morts sans sépulture* is not what it may appear at first: a melodramatic topical treatment of the torture of Resistance fighters. It is a series of tragic variations on the intolerable human divorce created by the presence of pain. Not only is each character confined to his terror, to his torment, and to his pride, but the glance of the person who has undergone torture becomes unbearable to the one who has been spared. Worst of all: How is one to bear the glance of an individual who has been tortured for our sake? "Must I have my nails torn out to become your friend again?" cries out one of the characters. The Sartrean hero develops an almost morbid jealousy of the victim, a paradoxical yearning for pain as a passport to brotherhood. Hugo, in *Les Mains sales,* knows that his new comrades will never forgive him for having been a well-fed child. "They will never accept me," he moans. There is the same feeling of rejection in *Le Diable et le bon Dieu*. Goetz tries in vain to take upon himself the suffering of his dying mistress, as he will try in vain to share the agony of the peasants. An impossibility that marks his bitter isolation ("Why do they always suffer so much more than I will ever suffer?"), but that leads to a further determination to break into the prison of the others. As early as in *La Chambre*, this desire to "break into" assumes an obsessive quality. Only here the compulsion has not yet taken on social and political overtones. Eve feels excluded from her husband's insanity. But she is determined to join him behind his wall. That, of course, is the meaning of her willful confinement to the sick man's room.

At this point one begins to see by what devious but also rigorous logic the Sartrean tragic figure seeks to leave his private cell, only to break into the cell of the other and ultimately into the collective prison of a given group. This attempt at penetrating into an imprisoned collectivity is the subject of *Les Mouches,* a play that was written and performed during the German Occupation, at a time when the concepts of prison and freedom were loaded with a tragic potential. It was impossible not to see a striking parallel between Sartre's city of Argos and the France of Vichy, defeated, guilt-ridden, and degradingly submissive. The play is studded with topical allusions. Orestes returns on a national holiday invented by the rulers to keep collective remorse alive. Aegisthus, like Pétain, is a collaborator. Pétain collaborates with Nazi tyranny and Aegisthus with the tyranny of Zeus. The flies are the very symbol of moral decay. But characteristically, the inhabitants are fond of their flies. The little idiot boy whose eyes are literally covered with flies smiles contentedly. For the flies, like a sterile remorse, can be paradoxically comfortable. In fact, the people of Argos like their running sores so much that they scratch them with their dirty nails to keep them festering. The city of Argos thus appears as the sordid city of *nonfreedom* and *nonresponsibility*. It is also the city of guilt. And Zeus the tyrant, whose nostrils are tickled by the stench of carrions, relishes the odor of guilt—for guilt and shame that blind men to the possibility of their own responsible action are the God's only hope of fighting man's freedom.

Orestes' desire to win the name of guilt stealer represents his attempt to enter into the prison of the collectivity, first to save himself from his own negative freedom, but ultimately, having found his roots, in order to rediscover the meaning of authentic freedom. To achieve this, to belong, he must first commit an irrevocable act: the murder of his mother. What matters is thus not the avenging of past crimes, as in Aeschylus' tragedy, but a binding and at the same time liberating enterprise, which Sartre metaphorically conveys through a whole series of prison images. At the beginning of the play, Orestes' "innocence" is like a wide moat separating him from the people of Argos. He stands, figuratively, *outside*. Looking at the city, he explains to Electra: "It fends me off with all its walls, with all its roofs, with all its locked doors." Orestes dreams of becoming more "weighty." He is attracted to Argos precisely because it is a city of suffering and heaviness. He wants to draw the city around him like a thick blanket and curl himself up in it. Elsewhere, he says to Electra who has just warned him that even if he stayed a hundred years, he would still be a stranger: "I must go down into the depths,

among you. For you are all living at the very bottom of a pit."
Finally, the breaking-into-the-prison is expressed in a language
of violence: "I'll turn into an ax and hew these obstinate walls
asunder, I'll rip open the bellies of those bigoted houses. . . . I'll
be a wedge driving into the heart of the city, like a wedge
rammed into the heart of an oak tree." The simple and perhaps
impossible aim is the dream of a human solidarity which would
liberate the individual from his false freedom and bind him to
the freedom of a solidary group: "To become a man among
men." And it is significant that Goetz, in *Le Diable et le bon
Dieu,* repeats Orestes' wish word for word: *"Je veux être un
homme parmi les hommes."* [9]

Though fundamentally relevant in psychological and social
terms, Sartre's prison imagery is closely woven into the philosophical texture of his works. And this not as an illustration but
as a metaphoric embodiment of a philosophical dilemma. Thus
literature, for Sartre, is never a vehicle for already crystallized
thoughts but an experience that probes into its own meaning.
Nothing is more revealing than Sartre's statement, made during
an interview, that he discovered and developed his concept of
freedom in the very process of writing *Les Mouches.* An explora-
tory exercise, literature for him does not describe a dilemma, it *is*
the dilemma. Or rather, to put it in Sartrean terms, it does not
describe a "situation," it *is* the "situation." And, of course, every
situation is a trap.

[9] *Théâtre* (Paris, 1947), p. 64; *Le Diable et le bon Dieu* (Paris, 1951),
p. 275.

And, to begin with, there is existence itself. For the raw experience of *Dasein*—of "being there"—is that never-ending ensnarement in a perpetual present that Sartre so brilliantly describes in *La Nausée*. By means of a diary method that adheres to the banal, fragmented, and essentially undramatic experience of unfiltered, uninterpreted reality, Sartre shows how Roquentin lives each moment as it weighs on him, in an opaque immediacy, caught in a permanent indetermination. The diary form becomes an exercise in discontinuity, as we the readers, as well as the narrator, become prisoners of a chronic present tense, which also marks a chronic disintegration. Pure existence is thus shown as innocent of meaning. The very imprisonment in the here and the now turns out to be a revelation of absurdity.

But this revelation, this nausea that is almost an ecstasy of horror, is also an apprenticeship in existential awareness. Roquentin discovers that existence is original contingency, that life is not justifiable in its essence, and that man is not only free—terrifyingly free—but, as it were, condemned to freedom. He does not have but *is* his freedom. It is a bitter lesson, a most uncomfortable one—for, if this is so, then there is no escape from this freedom, there being no one in this world to whom man could delegate a responsibility that he, and he alone, must bear. This relation between freedom and responsibility is the corner stone of Sartre's ethical construction. Like Heidegger, Sartre stresses the "intentional structure" of human awareness.[10] In a key passage of

[10] John D. Wild, "The New Empiricism," in *Sartre: A Collection of Critical Essays,* ed. Edith Kern (New York, 1962), p. 139. The chapter originally appeared in *The Challenge of Existentialism,* 1955.

*L'Etre et le Néant* entitled "Freedom and Responsibility," Sartre writes that "man, condemned to be free, carries the weight of the entire world on his shoulders." [11] The very alienation of man, according to Sartre, forces him into a value-creating role. Orestes —so Zeus tells him in *Les Mouches*—is not in his own home: he is an intruder, a foreign body in the world, "like a splinter in flesh, or a poacher in his lordship's forest." What Sartre means is that man has been thrown into this world that he did not create and did not want. But here he is, and only he can provide for himself the values whereby he can live. As Orestes puts it, "human life begins on the far side of despair."

The image of the trap—*"tout est piège"*—is thus potentially dynamic, in so far as man is condemned permanently to seek an exit. But first comes the awareness of being ensnared. *"Nous sommes drôlement coincés"* (Are we trapped!) says Frantz in *Les Séquestrés d'Altona*. But immediately he adds: "There must be an exit"—and he repeats this twice. Sartre himself, in his essay on the function of literature, asseverates that it is the writer's duty to unveil to man, in each concrete situation, his potential for action; that he must measure man's servitude only to help him transcend it. [12]

This view of "man-in-situation" is reflected in Sartre's literary precepts as well as in his practice, particularly his dramaturgy. In the very passage in which he calls for a new theater of entrapment, Sartre also calls for the end of the theater of "characters." "No more characters: protagonists are entrapped freedoms, like

[11] *L'Etre et le Néant*, p. 639.
[12] *Situations II*, pp. 311–12.

the rest of us. What exits are there? Each personage will be nothing but a choice of an exit and will be worth exactly the exit he chose." And in the passage quoted earlier ("each situation is a trap, there are walls everywhere"), Sartre adds: "I have expressed myself badly: there are no exits to *choose*. An exit has to be invented. And every one of us, by inventing his own exit, invents himself. Man is to be invented every day." [13]

What this means, in literary terms, is that the playwright as well as the novelist must turn away from conventional character study. Malraux, in his preface to *Le Temps du mépris,* had taken the bourgeois novelist to task for eternally exploring the so-called "inner world" of his protagonists. In his introductory essay for *Les Temps modernes,* Sartre also proclaims the death of the spirit of analysis that isolates human beings in their "differences" and immobilizes them in their pseudo-essences. For Sartre, just as for Malraux, a man is not what he hides but what he does. He is the sum total of his acts. It is the act that defines man. By his acts he creates himself. Thus man is neither subject nor object but an eternal project. This, in fact, is why Sartre scorns the omniscient type of novelist who assumes a God-like privilege of dissecting and explaining his characters. Sartre's heroes may find themselves in a trap, but it is not the trap of their psychology. Their actions are not the expression of what they are, but the means by which they become what they are not yet. A literature of *praxis,* Sartre calls it: one that does not describe or explain but that brings man face to face with his latest dilemma.

Sartre himself is temperamentally drawn to "impossible" situ-

[13] *Ibid.,* p. 313.

ations, as witnessed by the permanent conflict between his philosophical tenets and his political allegiances. Replying to objections raised by George Lukacs in *Existentialisme ou Marxisme,* Sartre explains the precise nature of this dilemma:

> We were convinced *simultaneously* that historical materialism supplied the only valid interpretation of history and that existentialism remained the only concrete approach to reality. I do not pretend to deny the contradictions in this attitude. . . . Many intellectuals, many students have experienced and are still experiencing the tension of this double exigency.[14]

Honesty here lies in the refusal to juggle away a difficulty or a contradiction. There is little doubt that Sartre also draws a measure of satisfaction from the tension of double exigencies. But, above all, Sartre welcomes the trap of any dilemma because in it alone can man take the full measure of his inventive and self-liberating potential. Sartre believes that, faced with the two alternatives of any dilemma, man will of a sudden discover a third possibility—a discovery that amounts to an act of creation. Few writers have been more keenly aware of the problematical nature of human existence and of the challenging difficulties man's confined freedom provided.

[14] "Questions de méthode," *Les Temps Modernes,* September, 1957, pp. 338–417. Reprinted in *Critique de la raison dialectique.*

# Supervising Committee,

## The English Institute, 1963

# The Program

## September 3 Through September 6, 1963

*Conferences*

I. TRANSFORMING THE AMERICAN SCENE: THE NINETIES AND AFTER
   *Directed by J. C. Levenson, University of Minnesota*
   1. JAMES AND THE NOVEL OF MANNERS
      *Laurence Holland, Princeton University*
   2. SANTAYANA AND THE ADEQUACY OF NATURALISM
      *Richard C. Lyon, University of North Carolina*
   3. ROBINSON'S MODERNITY
      *J. C. Levenson, University of Minnesota*
   4. EUGENE O'NEILL AND THE ESCAPE FROM THE CHATEAU D'IF
      *John Henry Raleigh, University of California at Berkeley*

II. IDEAS IN THE DRAMA
   *Directed by John Gassner, Yale University*
   1. SHAW ON IBSEN AND THE DRAMA OF IDEAS
      *John Gassner, Yale University*
   2. IDEAS IN THE PLAYS OF EUGENE O'NEILL
      *Edwin A. Engel, University of Michigan*
   3. BRECHT AND THE DRAMA OF IDEAS
      *Gerald Weales, University of Pennsylvania*
   4. SARTRE AND THE DRAMA OF ENSNAREMENT
      *Victor Brombert, Yale University*

III. SAMSON AGONISTES

*Directed by Joseph H. Summers, Washington University*
  (St. Louis)

  1. FROM SHADOWY TYPES TO TRUTH
  *William G. Madsen, Emory University*

  2. THE "DRY AND RUGGED" VERSE
  *Edward R. Weismiller, Pomona College*

  3. THE MOVEMENTS OF THE DRAMA
  *Joseph H. Summers, Washington University (St. Louis)*

IV. STUDY OF PROSODY

*Directed by James Craig LaDrière, Catholic University of*
  *America*

  1. LITERARY STUDY OF PROSODY
  *John Hollander, Yale University*

  2. VERSE AND LANGUAGES
  *John Lotz, Columbia University*

  3. VARIETIES OF ENGLISH VERSE
  *Winifred P. Lehmann, University of Texas*

*Evening Meeting, September 5*
  PRIVATE LETTERS TO A PUBLIC MONUMENT
  *W. H. Bond, Houghton Library, Harvard University*

# Registrants, 1963

Kenneth T. Abrams, Queens College; Ruth M. Adams, Douglass College; Gellert S. Alleman, Rutgers University; Marcia Allentuck, City College of New York; Lynn Altenbernd, University of Illinois; Reta Anderson, Emory University; L. M. Antalis, College of Steubenville; Mother Mary Anthony, Rosemont College; Ashur Baizer, Ithaca College; C. L. Barber, University of Indiana; Lynn C. Bartlett, Vassar College; Phyllis Bartlett Pollard, Queens College; Mary Dexter Bates, Ithaca College; David W. Becker, Miami University (Ohio); Alice R. Bensen, London; Sister Mary Berchman, Maria College; Whitney Blake, Oxford University Press; Sheila Blanchard, University of Rochester; Sister M. Bonaventure, Nazareth College; W. H. Bond, Harvard University; Edwin T. Bowden, University of Texas; Brother C. Francis Bowers, f.s.c., Manhattan College; Fredson Bowers, University of Virginia; John D. Boyd, s.j., Fordham University; Helene M. Brewer, Queens College; Mary Campbell Brill, Madison College; James Broderick, Bryn Mawr College; Reuben A. Brower, Harvard University; Robert M. Browne, Université de Montréal; Margaret Bryant, Brooklyn College; Mrs. W. Bryher, Vaud, Switzerland; Jean R. Buchert, University of North Carolina (Greensboro); Charles O. Burgess, Old Dominion College; Brother Fidelian Burke, f.s.c., La Salle College; Arthur Burkhard, Cambridge, Massachusetts; Mervin Butovsky, Sir George Williams University.

Grace J. Calder, Hunter College; Edward Callan, Western Michigan University; Kenneth Neill Cameron, The Carl H. Pforzheimer Library, New York; Oscar James Campbell, Columbia University; Norman Carlson, Western Michigan University; Leslie F. Chard, II, Emory University; Sister Mary Charles, Immaculate College; Maurice

M. Charney, Rutgers University; Hugh C. G. Chase, University of New Brunswick; Mother Madeleine Clary, College of New Rochelle; James L. Clifford, Columbia University; John Conley, Queens College; Brother Laurence Connoley, f.s.c., La Salle College; Francis X. Connolly, Fordham University; Albert Cook, State University of New York (Buffalo); John Coolidge, University of California (Berkeley); Roberta D. Cornelius, Randolph-Macon Woman's College; Max Cosman, Brooklyn, New York; G. Armour Craig, Amherst College; Martha A. Craig, Wellesley College; Lucille Crighton, Gulf Park College; James H. Croushore, Mary Washington College; J. V. Cunningham, Brandeis University; Reverend John Curry, Bellarmine College; Curtis Dahl, Wheaton College; Bob Darrell, Drew University; Charles T. Davis, Pennsylvania State University; Winifred M. Davis, The Carl H. Pforzheimer Library, New York; Leonard W. Deen, Queens College; Sara DeFord, Goucher College; Robert M. Dell, Pace College; Charlotte D'Evelyn, Mt. Holyoke College; John H. Dorenkamp, Holy Cross College; Georgia S. Dunbar, Hofstra University; Edgar H. Duncan, Vanderbilt University; I. L. M. Duncan, Belmont College; Mother Margaret Mary Dunn, Manhattanville College of the Sacred Heart; David A. Dushkin, Random House.

Edward R. Easton, Pace College; Ursula E. Eder, Brooklyn College; Mother Mary Eleanor, Rosemont College; Scott Elledge, Cornell University; Sister Elizabeth Marian, College of Mount St. Vincent; Newell W. Ellison, Oberlin College; Richard Ellmann, Northwestern University; Edwin A. Engel, University of Michigan; Martha Winburn England, Queens College; David V. Erdman, New York Public Library; Sister Marie Eugenie, Immaculata College; Doris V. Falk, Douglass College; Signi Falk, Coe College; H. Alfred Farrell, Lincoln University; Arthur Fenner, Jr., Catholic University of America; Lillian Fischer, Brooklyn College; Paul D. Fleck, University of Western Ontario; Edward G. Fletcher, University of Texas; F. Cudworth Flint, Dartmouth College; Sister Florence Anne, St. Vincent Ferrer High School; Claude R. Flory, Florida State University; Elizabeth S.

Foster, Oberlin College; Frances A. Foster, Vassar College; Richard L. Francis, Brown University; Edwin Fussell, Claremont Graduate School; Paul Fussell, Jr., Rutgers University; Edward L. Galligan, Western Michigan University; Dewey Ganzel, Oberlin College; H. R. Garvin, Bucknell University; John Gassner, Yale University; Malcolm Goldstein, Queens College; Sister Mary Gonzaga, Maria College; George Goodin, Holy Cross College; Anthony Gosse, Bucknell University; Sister Mary Grace, Rivier College; Richard L. Greene, Wesleyan University; M. E. Grenander, State University of New York (Albany); Allen Guttmann, Amherst College; Jean H. Hagstrum, Northwestern University; Victor M. Hamm, Marquette University; John B. Harcourt, Ithaca College; Katherine S. Harris, Queens College; John A. Hart, Carnegie Institute of Technology; Ann L. Hayes, Carnegie Institute of Technology; Miriam M. Heffernan, Brooklyn College; Donald S. Heine, Upsala College; Thelma J. Henner, Columbia University; John H. Hicks, University of Massachusetts; William Bernard Hill, s.j., Novitiate of St. Isaac Jogues; Frederick W. Hilles, Yale University; C. Fenno Hoffman, Jr., Rhode Island School of Design; Stanley M. Holberg, St. Lawrence University; Laurence B. Holland, Princeton University; Norman M. Holland, Massachusetts Institute of Technology; John Hollander, Yale University; Ward Hooker, Bucknell University; Vivian C. Hopkins, State University of New York (Albany); Edward Hubler, Princeton University; J. Paul Hunter, Williams College; Samuel Hynes, Swarthmore College.

Elizabeth Isaacs, Cornell College; Sears Jayne, Queens College; W. T. Jewkes, Pennsylvania State University; George W. Johnson, Temple University; R. J. Kaufmann, University of Rochester; Alfred L. Kellogg, Rutgers University; James G. Kennedy, Upsala College; Karl Kiralis, St. Lawrence University; H. L. Kleinfield, C. W. Post College; Edgar H. Knapp, Pennsylvania State University; Edwin B. Knowles, Pratt Institute; Stanley Koehler, University of Massachusetts; Katherine Koller, University of Rochester; J. Craig LaDrière, Catholic University of America; Sidney Lamb, Sir George Williams

University; Reverend Henry St. C. Lavin, s.j., Loyola College; Lewis Leary, Columbia University; W. P. Lehmann, University of Texas; J. C. Levenson, University of Minnesota; Oswald LeWinter, Columbia University; Nancy E. Lewis, Denison University; R. W. B. Lewis, Yale University; Ellen Douglass Leyburn, Agnes Scott College; Herman W. Liebert, Yale University; Jean S. Lindsay, Hunter College; Winslow H. Loveland, Boston University; Joseph P. Lovering, Canisius College; Richard C. Lyon, University of North Carolina; Marion K. Mabey, Wells College; Beatrice Clifford McDade, Purchase, New York; George McFadden, Temple University; Richard A. Macksey, The Johns Hopkins University; Elizabeth T. McLaughlin, Bucknell University; Hugh N. Maclean, State University of New York (Albany); Lorna E. Maclean, Sir George Williams University; William G. Madsen, Emory University; Mother C. E. Maguire, Newton College of the Sacred Heart; Kenneth B. Marshall, Denison University; Harold C. Martin, Harvard University; John Kelly Mathison, University of Wyoming; Donald C. Mell, Jr., Rutgers University; Vivian Mercier, City College of New York; Harrison T. Meserole, Pennsylvania State University; John H. Middendorf, Columbia University; Milton Millhauser, University of Bridgeport; Reverend Joseph G. Milunas, s.j., West Baden College; Sister Miriam Jane, Seton Hill College; Sister Jeanne Pierre Mittnisht, The College of Saint Rose; Mother Grace Monahan, College of New Rochelle.

William Nelson, Columbia University; Kenneth B. Newell, University of Kansas; Helaine Newstead, Hunter College; Eleanor Nicholes, Harvard College Library; Reverend William T. Noon, s.j., Fordham University; John Ogden, Ithaca College; Mother Elizabeth O'Gorman, Manhattanville College of the Sacred Heart; Reverend Joseph E. O'Neill, s.j., Fordham University; Mother Thomas Aquinas O'Reilly, College of New Rochelle; James M. Osborn, Yale University; Charles A. Owen, Jr., University of Connecticut; Edward Partridge, Bucknell University; Sister Marie Paula, College of Mount St. Vincent; Richard Pearce, Alfred University; Roy Harvey Pearce,

University of California (San Diego); Norman Holmes Pearson, Yale University; Kathryn King Pease, The Chapin School; Henry F. Pommer, Allegheny College; Abbie F. Potts, Rockford College; William C. Pratt, Miami University (Ohio); Robert Preyer, Brandeis University; Max Putzel, University of Connecticut; John Henry Raleigh, University of California (Berkeley); Isabel E. Rathborne, Hunter College; Mother Janet Reberdy, Manhattanville College of the Sacred Heart; John H. Reed, Ohio Wesleyan University; Mrs. Louise L. Reed, Ohio Wesleyan University; John P. Reesing, Jr., The George Washington University; Warner G. Rice, University of Michigan; Sister M. Rita Margaret, Caldwell College for Women; Edgar V. Roberts, Hunter College; Francis X. Roellinger, Oberlin College; Sister Rose Bernard Donna, College of St. Rose; Seymour Rudin, University of Massachusetts; Rebecca D. Ruggles, Brooklyn College; Sister St. Augustine, Rivier College; Henry W. Sams, Pennsylvania State University; Irene Samuel, Hunter College; Bernard Schilling, University of Rochester; Helene B. M. Schnabel, New York City; James Scholes, State University of New York (Geneseo); Flora Rheta Schreiber, The New School; Merton M. Sealts, Jr., Lawrence College; Frank Seward, The Catholic University of America; Richard Sexton, Fordham University; Ellenor Shannon, Denison University; John T. Shawcross, Douglass College; Robert G. Shedd, Ohio State University; Anne Talbot Shorter, Winston-Salem Teachers College; Robert Newland Shorter, Wake Forest College; Gerald Smith, State University of New York (Geneseo); Reverend Paul F. Smith, s.j., The Creighton University; Nelle Smither, Douglass College; Koji Sonoda, Teachers College, Columbia University; George Soule, Carleton College; J. Gordon Spaulding, University of British Columbia; Keith Stewart, McMicken College, University of Cincinnati; Maureen T. Sullivan, Albertus Magnus College; Joseph H. Summers, Washington University (St. Louis); Barbara Swain, Vassar College.

Michitoshi Tashiro, Yokohama Municipal University; Ruth Z. Temple, Brooklyn College; E. William Terwilliger, Ithaca College; Sister Thérèse, Trinity College (Washington); Jonathan Thomas,

Douglass College; Sister Thomas Marion, Nazareth College; Doris Stevens Thompson, Russel Sage College; Michael Timko, Queens College; Nancy Tischler, Susquehanna University; A. R. Towers, Jr., Queens College; Alan Trachtenberg, Pennsylvania State University; Winifred M. Van Etten, Cornell College; David M. Vieth, Hunter College; Sister M. Vincentia, Albertus Magnus College; Sister M. Vivien, Caldwell College for Women; Eugene M. Waith, Yale University; Andrew J. Walker, Georgia Institute of Technology; Aileen Ward, Sarah Lawrence College; Herbert S. Weil, Jr., University of Connecticut; Edward R. Weismiller, Pomona College; Jeanne K. Welcher, St. John's University; James J. Wey, University of Detroit; Mother E. White, Newton College of the Sacred Heart; Brother Joseph Wiesenfarth, La Salle College; Mother Margaret Williams, Manhattanville College of the Sacred Heart; W. K. Wimsatt, Jr., Yale University; James N. Wise, Newark College of Engineering; S. K. Workman, Newark College of Engineering; Marjorie G. Wynne, Yale University Library; James Dean Young, Georgia Institute of Technology; William H. Youngren, Massachusetts Institute of Technology.